The Life

The Life

Fifty-Two Lessons from the Life of Jesus

MIKE WILSON

WIPF & STOCK · Eugene, Oregon

THE LIFE
Fifty-Two Lessons from the Life of Jesus

Copyright © 2024 Mike Wilson. All rights reserved. Except for brief quotations in critical publications or reviews, no part of this book may be reproduced in any manner without prior written permission from the publisher. Write: Permissions, Wipf and Stock Publishers, 199 W. 8th Ave., Suite 3, Eugene, OR 97401.

Wipf & Stock
An Imprint of Wipf and Stock Publishers
199 W. 8th Ave., Suite 3
Eugene, OR 97401

www.wipfandstock.com

PAPERBACK ISBN: 979-8-3852-3096-9
HARDCOVER ISBN: 979-8-3852-3097-6
EBOOK ISBN: 979-8-3852-3098-3

VERSION NUMBER 11/06/24

Unless otherwise noted, all Scripture references are taken from Holy Bible, New Living Translation, copyrighted 1996 by Tyndale House Publishers. Used by permission.

Scripture quotations taken from the Holy Bible, New International Version®, NIV®. Copyright © 1973, 1978, 1984, 2011 by Biblica, Inc.™ Used by permission. All rights reserved worldwide.

Scripture quotations taken from the King James Version (KJV) are in the public domain.

Contents

Introduction | vii

1. The True Story of Jesus | 1
2. Make Room for Jesus | 6
3. Come Boldly to God | 9
4. Hoping Beats Wishing | 13
5. Motivated to Obey | 16
6. You Make God Happy | 19
7. Don't Be Alone | 23
8. Resist Temptation | 27
9. Fight Your Devils | 32
10. Follow Me | 36
11. God Will Make You | 40
12. Don't Forget to Feast | 44
13. God Blesses Hurting People | 49
14. Breaking the Chains of Father Wounds | 53
15. How to Pray | 58
16. Renewed by Grace | 62
17. Don't Build Offense | 66
18. Ask God for Good Gifts | 71
19. The Church Is a Rock | 75
20. Sinners Need Miracles | 80
21. God Has a Green Thumb | 83
22. How to Be Healed | 87

23 Be Made Whole | 91
24 Unlocking Blessings | 95
25 In His Hands | 100
26 Staying Faithful in Storms | 104
27 Embracing Sea Monsters | 108
28 Storm the Gates of Hell | 112
29 Be a Rock | 115
30 Don't Be a Satan | 119
31 His Glory and Grace | 123
32 Give Attention | 126
33 The Lies We Feel | 129
34 Open Your Doors | 132
35 Childlike Humility | 136
36 Waiting on Jesus | 140
37 Be Righteous | 145
38 Donkeys Beat Horses | 149
39 Throw Tables | 153
40 Christians Love | 158
41 Afraid of Antichrists | 162
42 The Money Test | 167
43 Commune | 170
44 Homecoming | 174
45 Who to Vote For | 178
46 Wear Christian T-Shirts | 183
47 But God Can | 187
48 God's Approval | 192
49 Play Infinite Games | 196
50 Bringing Zombies to Life | 200
51 Enduring Pain | 204
52 How to Be Powerful | 209

Conclusion | 213
Acknowledgments | 215
Bibliography | 217

Introduction

THE LIFE IS A journey through the life of Jesus in fifty-two chapters, each offering some background information and a helpful reflection. As we walk through the story of his life, from birth to ascension, we will explore the profound impact these events and teachings can have on our lives today.

This book is designed to be used as a devotional. Set aside ten minutes each week to read one chapter and the accompanying Scripture passage. The chapters can be read alone, apart from the accompanying Scripture passage, but reading them together will give greater understanding. Then spend the rest of the week praying and meditating on the insights gained. Ask God to renew your mind and build your strength through these reflections. If you miss a week, don't get discouraged. Simply pick up where you left off and continue your spiritual journey.

Jesus of Nazareth is undeniably the most influential person in human history. He entered a broken world and offered a remedy for its deepest wounds. If you allow him, Jesus will become the most influential person in your life, healing your deepest wounds and guiding you through your struggles. The Christian God is not a distant, indifferent deity. He entered his creation, becoming the lead character in the story he authored. This matters because his creation plan gives our lives meaning, and his presence offers us hope.

Jesus is much more than history's greatest teacher, an influential leader, and a miracle worker. He is the only way to eternal life. The remedy Jesus brought to the world was a sacrifice. He died the death we deserved to die for our sins. For those who accept it, Jesus is our substitutionary atonement:

> [God] wants everyone to be saved and to understand the truth.
> For there is one God and one Mediator who can reconcile God

Introduction

and humanity—the man Christ Jesus. He gave his life to purchase freedom for everyone. (1 Tim 2:3–6)

Jesus is the mediator between God and man. He is the great High Priest whose death and resurrection made us holy and gave us eternal life, making us worthy to be in the presence of God. As a result, the Holy Spirit lives within us.

> Since we have a great High Priest who has entered heaven, Jesus the Son of God, let us hold firmly to what we believe. This High Priest of ours understands our weaknesses, for he faced all of the same testings we do, yet he did not sin. So let us come boldly to the throne of our gracious God. There we will receive his mercy, and we will find grace to help us when we need it most. (Heb 4:14–16)

Jesus can relate to our pain. He was rejected, criticized, and hated. He felt physical pain, hunger, and exhaustion. He experienced anger, fear, doubt, and grief. Jesus even felt tempted to sin, but he never sinned. Learn from his life and teachings. Let him encourage you and help you grow in faith.

As you embark on this journey, my prayer is that you will experience profound hope and healing. May this book inspire you and give you the courage to become the person God created you to be. Through each chapter, let Jesus' life and teachings transform you, guiding you closer to him each week.

1

The True Story of Jesus

Accompanying Scripture Reading: Luke 1:1–5

Growing up, we are told a lot of stories. Some are good and some are not so good. Now that I have sons of my own, I've started telling them some of the stories I heard when I was a kid. I've noticed that many of them are not as good as I remember. For example: "Rock a bye baby on the tree top, When the wind blows the cradle will rock, When the bough breaks the cradle will fall, And down will come baby, cradle and all." Yes, we have been telling our children a story about a baby falling to her death. Maybe we should spend some time thinking about the stories we tell our kids.

One of my favorite childhood memories is when my mom read *Pilgrim's Progress* to my twin brother and me every night. Now, every day at dinner I read a story to my family from *The Jesus Storybook Bible*. When we read, we differentiate the fairy tales from the true stories that we read.

The true stories, especially the ones that describe God interacting with his creation, help us learn how we should live in the world in which he created us. My hope is that, for my kids, the Bible stories will be more than entertainment; that they will be the foundation on which we build our lives.

This is one reason Darci and I have chosen not to tell our kids that Santa Claus (as described in the modern-day fairy tales) or any other fictional character is real. We want our children to know that if we tell them something, it is the truth. If we tell them Santa is real and then they find out that he isn't, will they assume we also lied about Jesus? In a world where so many young people are leaving the Christian faith, I'm not willing to take the risk. We do, however, tell our children the story of Saint Nicholas who was a devout Christian who gave generously to those in need.

The greatest part of God's eternal story is the story of God entering the world he created. That part of the story begins in Bethlehem, a city that is now in the West Bank, a region of Israel governed by the Palestinians.

Luke begins his version of the story like this:

> When Herod was king of Judea. (Luke 1:5)

Luke was a historian and he went out of his way to show that this is no fairy tale. When Luke names Herod, he gives the reader a tool to understand the place and time of the events.

Then, in chapter 2, Luke gives us even more evidentiary tools:

> At that time the Roman emperor, Augustus, decreed that a census should be taken throughout the Roman Empire. (This was the first census taken when Quirinius was governor of Syria.) (Luke 2:1–2)

Jesus was an Israelite born in Israel. Why was the Roman emperor forcing Jews to participate in a census? Rome was an occupying force that used military power to force Jews to pay taxes to the government that conquered them. The current political unrest in Israel is distressing, but imagine if Iran, after attacking them, occupied the nation and forced the Jews to pay taxes to the enemy.

Luke's mention of King Herod, Caesar Augustus, and Governor Quirinius is more than just historical name-dropping; these were prominent political figures that readers in the first century would have immediately recognized. By referencing them, Luke firmly anchors the story of Jesus in real historical events, making it clear that this is no myth or legend but a true account grounded in history. Luke's name-dropping could be comparable to a historian writing a chapter in a history book in the early 1800s and including names like George Washington, Thomas Jefferson, Betsy Ross, or Paul Revere. Our history teachers made sure we knew who they were. To learn about important history, I have visited places like Colonial Williamsburg, Mount Vernon, and Gettysburg. For the same reason, I've visited Bethlehem, Jerusalem, and Jericho. No respected historian denies the existence of Jesus, and we are convinced by the life that he lived that Jesus was more than a man or a prophet. God showed up in human history.

From what we know of Augustus, it would not have been surprising for him to require a census, but the biblical record recorded in Luke 2 is the only evidence of this census:

> All returned to their own ancestral towns to register for this census. And because Joseph was a descendant of King David, he had to go to Bethlehem in Judea, David's ancient home. He traveled there from the village of Nazareth in Galilee. (Luke 2:3–4)

If you've read the story of the great King David, you probably remember that David was a shepherd in Bethlehem before he was the king of Israel, and because Joseph was a descendant of David, he had to go to Bethlehem for the census.

> He took with him Mary, to whom he was engaged, who was now expecting a child. (Luke 2:5)

You might wonder why Joseph didn't go alone to Bethlehem. Why did he take Mary with him? He might have done it because he wanted to be with Mary when she gave birth, or perhaps Mary went with Joseph because she knew that Micah's prophecy must be fulfilled:

> But you, O Bethlehem Ephrathah, are only a small village among all the people of Judah. Yet a ruler of Israel, whose origins are in the distant past, will come from you on my behalf. (Mic 5:2)

Micah's prophecy was written almost eight hundred years before Jesus was born, and because Mary went with Joseph, Micah's prophecy was fulfilled. The fulfillment of prophecy is one of many reasons we believe Jesus is the Messiah.

If Jesus really is who he said he is, that truth should revolutionize every aspect of our lives. It's not something we can simply hear and then set aside; it's a call to action that demands a response. Believing Jesus isn't just a fairy-tale character but the living Savior means recognizing his authority, embracing his teachings, and allowing his presence to transform our hearts and minds. This belief compels us to reorient our priorities, values, and actions to align with his will, because when we acknowledge the reality of who Jesus is, it changes everything.

When individuals truly embrace the truth of who Jesus is, their lives are changed in profound ways—reflecting his love, grace, and truth in their actions and decisions. Then, as these transformed lives come together, they create a ripple effect that can influence families, neighborhoods, and even nations. Belief in Jesus has the power to change us and it reshapes entire communities and societies. The gospel is not just a personal message but a call to collective action, challenging us to live out our faith in ways that bring healing, justice, and hope to the world around us. The power of belief in Jesus is a force that, when fully embraced, can revolutionize the world.

In fact, the life of Jesus has already profoundly influenced history, not only as a religious figure but as a catalyst for moral and social change throughout the centuries. His teachings on love, compassion, forgiveness, and justice have shaped the ethical foundations of countless societies and inspired movements for human rights, social justice, and peace. From the early Christian communities that transformed the Roman Empire to the abolition of slavery and the civil rights movement, the impact of Jesus' life is evident in the ongoing pursuit of a more just and compassionate world. Recognizing Jesus as a real, historical figure is essential, as it affirms the tangible and lasting influence he has had on the course of history and continues to have today.

The apostle John also recorded the historical events of Jesus' life, but he did so as an eyewitness to the events:

> We proclaim to you the one who existed from the beginning, whom we have heard and seen. We saw him with our own eyes and touched him with our own hands. He is the Word of life. This one who is life itself was revealed to us, and we have seen him. And now we testify and proclaim to you that he is the one who is eternal life. He was with the Father, and then he was revealed to us. We proclaim to you what we ourselves have actually seen and heard so that you may have fellowship with us. And our fellowship is with the Father and with his Son, Jesus Christ. We are writing these things so that you may fully share our joy. (1 John 1:1–4)

John wrote down what he saw so that these events could change your life, allowing you to experience the joy of following Jesus. Although we may not have the opportunity to physically spend time with Jesus as the apostles did, John does everything he can to help us understand that the life of Christ should be the central truth of our lives. The question remains: Do you know the joy of having an eternal relationship with Jesus?

Reflect: If you were fully convinced that Jesus is who he said he is, what part of your life would change the most?

2

Make Room for Jesus

Accompanying Scripture Reading: Luke 2:1–20

I'VE HAD THE POWERFUL experience of visiting the cave under the Church of the Nativity in Bethlehem, where you can stand in the place believed to be the birthplace of Jesus. While some might be skeptical of this claim, thinking Jesus was born in a barn, that's likely not the case. The tradition of a barn stems from Luke 2:7, where it mentions that Jesus was placed in a manger—a feeding trough for animals. However, this doesn't necessarily mean he was born in a barn. In that time, it was common for animals to be kept in homes or caves for their safety and care.

Others question the authenticity of the Church of the Nativity, doubting how such history could be accurately preserved without modern maps. But consider this: If a well-known figure like Donald Trump visited a restaurant in Gillette, Wyoming (where he is very popular), that restaurant would proudly display a sign proclaiming "Donald Trump ate here." This is similar to the way many of the locations associated with Jesus have been preserved. Generation after generation would tell their children, "This is where Jesus _____," filling in the blank with a significant event. Additionally, throughout history, occupying forces would sometimes build structures over these significant sites in an attempt to obscure their importance. Ironically, these actions often served to create lasting monuments to the very events they sought to erase. If the Messiah was born in your home, you would likely boast about it often, perhaps even turning it into a tourist attraction—or at least setting up a gift shop.

Last year, there was an early release day at my son Lincoln's school, and Lincoln's terrible parents didn't realize it. So, he had to sit out in the snow and wait for us to pick him up. Eventually a teacher walked up to Lincoln and asked, "Did your parents forget you?" He said, "Yeah." She asked, "What's your name? I'll go call them." Lincoln said, "You know who I am." "No, I don't. What's your name?" "You know my name . . . I'm famous." He got his ego from his mom.

The title "Messiah" or "Christ" would have made Jesus famous in ancient Israel, but Jesus wasn't famous when he was born. God's Son deserved to be born in a castle, but his beginning was humble. The true story of Jesus' birth is the story of a baby who was laid in a manger because his father's relatives failed to prepare a room for his family:

> [Mary] laid [Jesus] in a manger, because there was no lodging available for them. (Luke 2:7)

Because there was no room for Jesus in the house, he was born among the animals. Mary's family went home for the holiday and their family didn't prepare them room. The famous Christmas song "Joy to the World" says, "Joy to the world, the Lord is come!/ Let earth receive her King!/ Let every heart prepare Him room."[1] So, do we?

What does your Christmas schedule look like? In the Christmas season, do we focus primarily on Christ? Or do we fill our time with parties, shopping, and movies? It's wise for us to choose to not over-indulge on the things of this world so there is room to focus on Christ. Don't wake up in the new year overly lethargic and tired because you bought all the stuff and ate all the stuffing. Don't overeat in December because you plan to diet in January. Instead, prepare him room.

---

1. Watts, "Joy to the World."

I love how the song is worded: "prepare Him room." That phrase is so much better than "make room for him." "Make room" is a phrase that implies shoving everything to the side so that you can fit one more thing in. "Prepare room" is a phrase that implies a plan and a schedule. To prepare room for something, you will likely have to get rid of something else.

Many people who call themselves a "Christian" make at least a little room for Jesus in their lives. They want just enough Jesus to have an easier life. They think, "Okay God, I can squeeze you in. I'll just pray on my way to work in the morning. I don't need church or any of that other 'organized religion' stuff."

John the Baptist told the world to prepare him room:

Prepare the way for the Lord. (Matt 3:2)

It's not enough to prepare some time in your schedule for a weekly chat with God. He wants us to prepare room in our hearts, to love him and sacrifice for him. Let every heart prepare him room. It's about your heart. So many people recognize a need to have Jesus in their lives, but their hearts are so full of the worries of this world, they don't have time to think about heaven. They don't make room for Jesus because they think this life is all there is, but this life is not all there is.

Preparing room for Jesus isn't just a seasonal task—it's a lifelong commitment. It requires intentionality and dedication to clear out the distractions and clutter that often fill our hearts and minds. This might mean re-evaluating our priorities, letting go of worldly pursuits, or making sacrifices to ensure that Jesus remains at the center of our lives. By consciously preparing room for him, we open ourselves to experiencing the fullness of his love, peace, and purpose.

Someday, you will stand before God to be judged. If he has to judge you based on how good you are, you will be found guilty. However, if you make room for Jesus in your heart, if you invite him in, then on judgment day you won't be judged based on your goodness. You will be judged based on Jesus' goodness. God will see that you are in relationship with Jesus, and you will be forgiven, forgiven for everything. Will you prepare room in your heart for Jesus today?

Reflect: Are there areas of your life that have not yet been surrendered to God?

3

Come Boldly to God

Accompanying Scripture Reading: Matthew 2:1–12

When visualizing the Christmas nativity scene, we usually picture Mary and Joseph, some shepherds, and three wise men looking down at baby Jesus. However, the truth is we don't know if there were three wise men. We say there were three because they brought three gifts to Jesus' parents. However, we do know that these wise men, however many there were, were highly educated. They were also very wealthy, and they were desperate to meet this little boy who might be the great Messiah for whom the Jews had been waiting:

> When they saw the star, they were filled with joy! They entered the house and saw the child with his mother, Mary, and they bowed down and worshiped him. Then they opened their treasure

The Life

chests and gave him gifts of gold, frankincense, and myrrh. (Matt 2:10–11)

Notice that the wise men went to a *house*. Matthew says the wise men went to a house because Jesus was likely two years old when they finally got there. They weren't in the stable anymore.

What do you give your two-year-olds for Christmas? I'm guessing you don't give them gold, frankincense, and myrrh, but the family would have been thankful for these gifts because they were both valuable and useful. With these gifts, these wise men, these very educated men, were foreshadowing what Jesus would become. Each gift implied a role that Jesus would play in his life:

- The gold foreshadowed the kingship of Jesus. They were proclaiming that Jesus is King!
- With the frankincense they announced Jesus as the great High Priest. Priests in the Jewish sacrificial system had two primary responsibilities: they prayed prayers on behalf of the people to God, and sacrificed animals to God for the forgiveness of sins.
- With the myrrh they demonstrated that Jesus was the lamb of God. In their day, myrrh was used to embalm dead bodies. This foreshadowed Jesus' death, his sacrifice.

Under the old covenant, an animal was killed as a sacrifice to God so that God would forgive the sins of the people, because for all of history there have been two opposing forces: the holiness of God and the sinfulness of men.

We live in a world that doesn't believe in sin. People believe we can all pick our truth, and if we believe something is moral, it is. They say, "What's true for you is true for you. If it makes you feel good, do it." So ask yourself, "Who says what is right and what is wrong?"

Someone once said the concept of sin is an outdated way of tricking kids into being good. Have you heard of the Elf on the Shelf? It's a little stuffed doll that you put on a shelf in your house. According to the superstition, he'll watch your kids and report their behavior to Santa. He's a spy. Who needs "sin" when Santa's "making a list, checking it twice"?

If we don't understand the holiness of God, we will always have a casual approach to sin. God hates sin because it separates us from him. God is perfect and we are sinful. For that reason, we can't be in relationship with

God unless someone is punished. Everything about God is perfect, so we can't be in his life, because we are not perfect. Holiness isn't simply one of God's attributes. It's the perfection of all his attributes. Everything about him and around him is holy. The problem is, we're not, unless he makes us holy.

In the Jewish sacrificial system, every year on Yom Kippur (the Day of Atonement), the high priest goes into the holiest place in the temple, burns frankincense to create smoke that represents a prayer of repentance from the people, and sacrifices a spotless lamb. The innocent lamb dies so that the guilty people can be forgiven and that's just weird. They kill cute little sheep for their own sins? It's gross and unfair, but God wants us to know how terrible sin is.

God is perfectly just and he wants us to know that sin has consequences. We may suffer because of our dumb decisions or it may be someone else that suffers. But sin always causes pain. The good news is that God is not only just, he's also merciful. The sacrificed animal temporarily satisfied God's justice and, at the same time, it extended mercy. We thank God that things have changed. Our high priest doesn't kill lambs anymore. We live under the new covenant, and the new covenant says Christ's single death was enough:

> For God's will was for us to be made holy by the sacrifice of the body of Jesus Christ, once for all time. Under the old covenant, the priest stands and ministers before the altar day after day, offering the same sacrifices again and again, which can never take away sins. But our High Priest offered himself to God as a single sacrifice for sins, good for all time. (Heb 10:10–12)

Jesus is the great High Priest, and he was sacrificed one time for all sins. Jesus sacrificed his perfection, his holiness, so that you could have it!

> Since we have a great High Priest who has entered heaven, Jesus the Son of God, let us hold firmly to what we believe. This High Priest of ours understands our weaknesses, for he faced all of the same testings we do, yet he did not sin. (Heb 4:14–15)

I hope you know that whatever you're going through, Jesus understands. He relates to our trials. He empathizes with our pain.

If you feel overwhelmed, know that in the garden of Gethsemane, Jesus said he was overwhelmed to the point of death.

- Have you ever had family problems? Jesus did. Jesus' family had crazy people just like your family does. And if you don't know who the crazy person in your family is, it's you. Jesus' family called him crazy.
- Have you felt judged? Jesus was conceived out of wedlock to a teenage mom. In his time, that was incredibly scandalous. Jesus lived in poverty, as a bastard's son.
- Have you ever been tempted to do something you didn't want to do? The satan attacked Jesus in a desert when he was weak and vulnerable.
- Have you ever had to endure the death of a loved one? Jesus had to experience the death of his best friend and his dad.
- Have you ever been betrayed by a friend? Jesus was betrayed by one of his best friends, and he was killed for a crime he didn't commit.
- Have you ever felt like God abandoned you? Jesus hung alone on the cross and cried out, "God why have you left me alone up here to die?" God is so holy that he even had to look away from his own son because of all the sin that was laid on him.

> The Word became human and made his home among us. He was full of unfailing love and faithfulness. (John 1:14)

Jesus came to live a hard life so that the great High Priest could relate to us. He wanted to have a relationship with us, and the best relationships are built on shared experiences.

> Let us come boldly to the throne of our gracious God. There we will receive his mercy, and we will find grace to help us when we need it most. (Heb 4:16)

You can come to him because he cares. He understands! Come to him boldly as you are. In fact, you don't have to run to him for him to see you. He can see you where you are and he's running to you. He's praying for you. In your weakness, his strength is perfect, so he came to you.

Reflect: How should knowing that God knows us so completely change the way we live?

4

Hoping Beats Wishing

Accompanying Scripture Reading: Matthew 2:1-18

WE'VE ALL FOUND OURSELVES stuck in life. Maybe we have a habit that's beyond a New Year's resolution fix. Maybe we've gotten a divorce, had a moral failure, or just felt purposeless. So, the question is: How is a life made new? Our first instinct is to try harder, to ask friends and family for help, or to give up, but none of those are the best option. The way to a better life is to put your faith in Jesus to give you what you cannot get on your own. If we put our faith in Jesus, he will make our lives new. He will lead us on a journey of becoming the people he created us to be. It will be rocky. There will be setbacks but he will continually renew us.

> Now faith is confidence in what we hope for and assurance about what we do not see. (Heb 11:1 NIV)

Faith is confidence. I am confident I've put my faith in the most logical worldview, the most logical explanation for the existence of the world.

The world likes to conflate two different kinds of faith. First, there's the real kind of faith that the Bible talks about. That's when you trust in something for a certain reason. The world believes everything came from nothing. I believe everything came from something. Which one sounds more logical to you? I am confident there's a God and that confidence gives me hope. In other words, faith gives me hope. If I trust God, I hope that he has a good plan for me. If I trust my wife, I have hope we're going to live a good life together. If I trust the chair I'm sitting in, I have logical hope that it's not going to break.

The second kind of faith is blind faith. There is a reason you have to add the word "blind." This is a different kind of faith than what we have as Christians. Our faith is not blind. We have evidence of what we put our faith in. When our faith is blind, it doesn't give us hope. When we don't have hope, we have to settle for a wish. But does wishing on a star accomplish anything? No. Wishes are unreal.

My sons and I just watched a Disney movie called *Wish*. While I did enjoy the movie, the main message of it was concerning. The movie encourages you to wish upon a star, but here's the kicker: it also says you are the star you should wish upon. If you listen to the theme song of the movie, you will notice that it perfectly sums up the materialistic worldview. That song is as religious as any song I've heard in church. It's a song about a god and that god is you. It says you are your own origin story.

Throughout history, facts have remained the same, but our understanding of those facts and our confident proclamations of those facts are often wrong. When it comes to the origin of life, the facts proclaimed by Scripture often contradict the facts proclaimed by many scientists. Here's an example: According to the American Museum of Natural History, scientists agree that you are stardust.[1] What does that mean about you? If you are only an accident of some star explosion, you cannot logically have hope.

> I pray that God, the source of hope, will fill you completely with joy and peace because you trust in him. Then you will overflow with confident hope through the power of the Holy Spirit. (Rom 15:13)

---

1. "We Are Stardust."

Hoping Beats Wishing

Jesus came to give us hope, not to grant our wishes. We think that getting what we want will make us happy, so we wish to win the lottery or to have our fantasies play out, but God gives us a hope that is much greater.

When it comes to Christmas presents, my kids have their hopes up. If there was ever a Christmas that did not come with presents, they would be completely blindsided. Why? Because even though they don't have the presents yet, they have faith in me. Based on their past experiences with me, they trust me.

> Let us hold tightly without wavering to the hope we affirm, for
> God can be trusted to keep his promise. (Heb 10:23)

The wise men didn't wish on a star. They followed a star. Why? Because they had faith that the star would lead them to the Messiah, and their faith was based on evidence. They had seen God's faithfulness in the past. They were familiar with his power and omnipotence.

At one point, the prophet Daniel was the leader of the order these wise men came from, and we assume he had read Num 24:17 to the ancestors of these wise men:

> I perceive him, but far in the distant future. A star will rise from
> Jacob; a scepter will emerge from Israel. (Num 24:17)

The prophet Daniel would have told the wise men to watch for a star. The wise men had faith that there would be a star because Daniel's prophecies had come true before. So, when they saw the star, they followed the star.

My prayer for you is that you will put your faith in Jesus so that he can produce hopeful joy in your life. God has been faithful in your past and he will be faithful in your future. He does not lie, and he holds the whole world in his hands.

Like the wise men did, when you put your faith in God, you don't wish on God to get things from him. Instead, you follow him, and that is how we're made new. Not by getting things from God, but by following him.

Reflect: Are you completely convinced God has good things planned for your life?

5

Motivated to Obey

Accompanying Scripture Reading: Luke 2:39–52

Jesus was a real man with real parents and real human problems.

Deuteronomy 16:16 says that every year, men in Israel celebrate three festivals: the Festival of Unleavened Bread, the Festival of Harvest, and the Festival of Shelters. During these events, every man must present himself before the Lord at the chosen place, ensuring that they bring a gift for the Lord and not come empty-handed.

The Festival of Unleavened Bread is also known as Passover. The Festival of Harvest is also known as Pentecost. The Festival of Shelters is also known as the Feast of Tabernacles, and Jewish men were required by Mosaic law to travel to Jerusalem three times a year for these three celebrations. As a result, Jesus' parents often traveled to Jerusalem. In addition, some rabbis insisted that women should also observe the law. Jewish males became accountable to the Mosaic law at the age of twelve. So this is the first time Jesus would have been required to attend the Passover celebration:

> Every year Jesus' parents went to Jerusalem for the Passover festival. When Jesus was twelve years old, they attended the festival as usual. After the celebration was over, they started home to Nazareth, but Jesus stayed behind in Jerusalem. His parents didn't miss him at first, because they assumed he was among the other travelers. But when he didn't show up that evening, they started looking for him among their relatives and friends. (Luke 2:41–44)

If you're a parent and you've ever lost a child, you have an idea of what Mary and Joseph were feeling in this moment. However, their shoulders felt the added weight of protecting the Messiah. I am sure they prayed in that moment, and we can only guess what they prayed. It was probably something like, "Um, God, we lost your son."

After celebrating the Passover festival, Jesus' friends and family would have made the long journey home from Jerusalem. People in a community would typically travel together in a caravan. They did this primarily for safety from thieves. As a result, Mary and Joseph assumed Jesus was safe in the caravan, but when they discovered Jesus was missing, they rushed back to Jerusalem:

> When they couldn't find him, they went back to Jerusalem to search for him there. Three days later they finally discovered him in the Temple, sitting among the religious teachers, listening to them and asking questions. All who heard him were amazed at his understanding and his answers. His parents didn't know what to think. "Son," his mother said to him, "why have you done this to us? Your father and I have been frantic, searching for you everywhere." "But why did you need to search?" he asked. "Didn't you know that I must be in my Father's house?" (Luke 2:45–49)

Jesus' family expected him to obey his parents. The fifth of the Ten Commandments is "honor your father and mother" (Ex 20:12). Because we know Jesus never sinned, we know that Jesus' actions were not intended to dishonor his parents. Jesus was in his Father's house. He wasn't lost at all. He was being obedient to his Father—his Heavenly Father.

Those who study the science of motivation have come up with an equation to explain motivation: motivation equals expectancy plus value minus cost.[1] Expectancy is the belief that you can do a behavior and achieve

---

1. Tix, "Science of Motivating Others."

a result. Value is the perception that a task is rewarding or useful. Cost is the sense that what you're doing causes some kind of pain.

People who don't exercise have used this equation to choose not to exercise. The cost (or pain) of getting up early and sweating is a bigger negative than the value (or reward) that they believe they will receive. In addition, they likely have low expectancy (or belief in their ability to succeed). In every moment, Jesus was motivated to do God's will. Jesus was fully human but he never sinned. He never missed the mark. He never did anything short of God's best. Everything he did pleased God.

When we become Christians, we are adopted into a family. God becomes our father. Although we cannot remain motivated to do God's will in every moment, we can pursue that goal.

Jesus expected he could accomplish what God wanted him to do. He believed that there was great value in doing God's will, and he knew that the reward was bringing glory to God. He knew there would be a cost, that there would be pain, but the reward and his belief that he could achieve what was being asked of him was always greater.

So why do we fail? We sabotage ourselves by believing the lies of the satan. The satan tells us that we can't do what is being asked of us, but the truth is God can accomplish it through us.

> For I can do everything through Christ, who gives me strength. (Phil 4:13)

The satan tells us the cost is too great, and yes, the cost is great. Even Jesus reminded us that the cost is great:

> Don't begin until you count the cost. (Luke 14:28)

> And everyone who has given up houses or brothers or sisters or father or mother or children or property, for my sake, will receive a hundred times as much in return and will inherit eternal life. (Matt 19:29)

Reflect: If God's will for our lives is superior to our will, why are we so tempted to ignore his instructions?

6

You Make God Happy

Accompanying Scripture Reading: Matthew 3

ALL OF US LIKE to be told we are doing a good job. I get discouraged if I feel that my work is going unnoticed or unappreciated, and I would be a better boss if I would remember to tell my employees they are doing well more often. So why don't I? Because I am too stingy with my "good jobs." My standards and expectations are too high. People have to work too hard to impress me. This is my problem, not theirs.

However, that is not the case with my sons. I must admit that I am one of those dads who thinks his sons are the best at everything. I constantly tell them how proud I am of them. Why do I do this? Because my love for them is not dependent on their success. My love for them is unconditional.

Today we are going to look at one of the few stories that appear in all four Gospels: Matthew, Mark, Luke, and John. In this story, God the Father tells Jesus, his Son, that he is proud of him. The Holy Spirit makes an appearance in this story too. All three persons of the Trinity were in the same place at the same time. That's not something that happens often in the Bible.

In Matt 3:11–14, John the Baptist explains that while he baptizes with water for repentance, someone greater than him is approaching. This exceptional figure, far superior to John, will baptize with the Holy Spirit and fire. He will have the capacity to separate the righteous from the unrighteous, likened to separating wheat from chaff with a winnowing fork. Jesus then arrives at the Jordan River to be baptized by John, who, recognizing Jesus' superiority, initially objects, feeling unworthy to baptize the Messiah.

John had just told the people that Jesus was going to be the ultimate baptizer. I imagine John was thinking, "Jesus, you're embarrassing me! I just told them you're the Messiah, now you want to be baptized with all of us sinners?"

> But Jesus said, "It should be done, for we must carry out all that God requires." (Matt 3:15)

There were three reasons Jesus needed to be baptized by John:

1. Prophecy

When we discussed the birth of Jesus, we talked about Jesus' birth in Bethlehem as fulfillment of a prophecy from the prophet Micah. These two stories include two of the more than three hundred prophecies that Jesus fulfilled in his life. It appears that Jesus often knew what he should do because God's prophets said the Messiah would do them.

> Listen! It's the voice of someone shouting, "Clear the way through the wilderness for the Lord! Make a straight highway through the wasteland for our God! Fill in the valleys, and level the mountains and hills. Straighten the curves, and smooth out the rough places. Then the glory of the Lord will be revealed, and all people will see it together. The Lord has spoken!" (Isa 40:3–5)

2. Obedience

Many times, Jesus did what he did because his heavenly Dad told him to do those things, and Jesus intentionally obeyed his Father's instructions.

When my sons ask me why I have given them an instruction, I generally try to give them a logical explanation. I want to help them learn to make good decisions, but I also want them to learn to obey even when they don't understand why I have told them to do something.

3. Inauguration

Jesus' baptism marked the beginning of his public, human ministry. It would culminate with Holy Week, when Jesus would go to the cross and rise from the tomb, but it started here. Similarly, when we are baptized, we announce to the world the beginning of a new life. Baptism is a testimony of who we are and who are we are becoming. It does not save us from the consequences of our sins, but it announces to the world that we have been saved.

If Jesus wanted to, he could have chosen a drastically different way to inaugurate his ministry. He could have used an army of angels to take the king's throne. He could have preached a fiery sermon. He could have caused a tornado to destroy the temple, or he could have ridden a unicorn into Rome. But Jesus chose baptism.

In going into the water for baptism, Jesus identified with people in their need for a savior. When we are baptized, we metaphorically place our life in the hands of the baptizer. We need the pastor to lift us out of the watery grave. As we are pulled from the water, we are resurrected to life.

Jesus was and is the King of kings and the Lord of lords, but how does he act as that King and Lord? What is the right thing for him to do? He lowers himself, lifts others up, and loves them. He is humble. Baptism is the perfect start for this kind of king. So, John wisely chose to go along with God's plan.

> After his baptism, as Jesus came up out of the water, the heavens were opened and he saw the Spirit of God descending like a dove and settling on him. (Matt 3:16)

Since our second son was born, Darci and I often divide and conquer. For example, at bedtime, she puts one son to bed and I put the other son to bed. However, occasionally we team up. On those days we put each son to bed together, and it is amazing to me how much they love that. The bond that they feel when our family comes together in that moment overwhelms them with emotion. It is not difficult for me to see this intimacy at Jesus' baptism. The three persons of God are united in this moment in perfect love. The Father smiles as the Spirit puts his hands on the shoulders of the Son:

> And a voice from heaven said, "This is my dearly loved Son, who brings me great joy." (Matt 3:17)

No matter if it's a mom affirming her child, a respected manager sharing a good word with an employee, or a husband sharing his heart with his wife, we all long for the affirming moments when we are told we are loved and appreciated. Who in your life needs some affirmation and encouragement? We need to learn from God in this moment. What is the godly thing to do? Let people know you value them; that you care about them; that they matter.

When we participate in baptism, either our baptism or the baptism of other Christians, we too are united with God. The apostle John (not the same guy as John the Baptist) calls us sons of God when he describes God's unconditional love for us:

> See how very much our Father loves us, for he calls us his children, and that is what we are! (1 John 3:1)

Christians, the same voice that expressed unearned love for Jesus is proclaiming his love for you today because you are his child.

Reflect: Is there anything that can periodically cause you to doubt God's love for you, and what can you do to avoid that doubt?

7

Don't Be Alone

Accompanying Scripture Reading: Matthew 3:13–17

THE STORY OF JESUS is one of a Son who loves his Father. The intimacy between the Father and the Son sustains the Son throughout his life. This is why it is so hard to read about how Jesus felt abandoned by God on the cross. They exist eternally in perfect unity, and in the moment of his Son's greatest pain, the Father had to turn his back on him.

> After his baptism, as Jesus came up out of the water, the heavens were opened and he saw the Spirit of God descending like a dove and settling on him. And a voice from heaven said, "This is my dearly loved Son, who brings me great joy." (Matt 3:16–17)

These verses are important because it's not often that we get a picture of all the persons of the Trinity together in the same place at the same time. The one true God is three eternal persons: the Father, the Son, and the Holy

Spirit. They are not the same person but they are all one God. They are not each one-third God. They are all entirely God and they have all lived eternally. This is probably the most difficult doctrine to understand because it's not humanly possible, but it's not necessary for it to be humanly possible.

God is the infinite creator. He is greater than humanity. If the creation could understand God, we would have a reason to doubt if he truly is the creator. When God created humans, he limited us to one person per soul, one person per being. He did not put the same limitation on himself. Similarly, Jesus chose to be fully God and fully man at the same time, and he can do that because he is not limited as we are.

In this incredible scene, we see the love that each person of the Trinity has for the other. You've probably heard 1 John 4:8, "God is love." God is love because God is a relationship. And how does God do relationships? Sacrificially. So, what does that mean for us? It can teach us about marriage (two people becoming one). It can teach us about mature love, sacrificial love, and so much more. Have a conversation with your loving Heavenly Father today.

Now, bear with me. I am going to give you a theological description of the Trinity and then I am going to explain why it matters to you. Understanding the Trinity can help us live better lives.

Humans were created in the image of God:

> God said, "Let us make human beings in our image, to be like us. They will reign over the fish in the sea, the birds in the sky, the livestock, all the wild animals on the earth, and the small animals that scurry along the ground." (Gen 1:26)

We were created to rule over the world. We are not equal to animals.

Notice that God uses the plural word "us," not the singular word "me." Who is he talking about? John 1 tells us that he is talking about the three persons of the Trinity. The triune God exists eternally in perfect unity within the godhead. Now, let me explain some aspects of how these persons exist together.

1. The Son is eternally begotten of the Father:

    > The king proclaims the Lord's decree: "The Lord said to me, 'You are my son. Today I have become your Father.'" (Ps 2:7)

    Jesus is eternal but he comes from the Father.

Don't Be Alone

2. The Spirit is eternally preceding from the Father and the Son:

> But I will send you the Advocate—the Spirit of truth. He will come to you from the Father and will testify all about me. (John 15:26)

3. The Holy Spirit is given by the Son from the Father.

Genesis tells us that the triune God made man in his image and that means it is not good for us to be alone. Why? If we are created in God's image, we are not created to be alone because God is not alone:

> Then the Lord God said, "It is not good for the man to be alone. I will make a helper who is just right for him." (Gen 2:18)

If you have ever felt the pain of loneliness, you experienced pain because you were living a reality in which you were not created to live. We were created to live in eternal fellowship.

So, to solve this problem, God took a rib from the man's side and created a woman. Like the Father and the Son, the woman comes from the man. Then, like the Spirit coming from the Father and Son, children precede from the union of the man and woman. It is not good for people to be alone.

When we unite with someone in marriage, we are meant to be two persons but entirely united. We are united financially, relationally, intimately, socially, and in every other aspect of life. There should be no separation or secrets between us.

When my wife and I got married, I was surprised by a feeling I did not think I would have. I imagined that we would get married and then wait a few years to have children. However, after we got married, I immediately started to develop a desire to add children to our family. It was as if I wanted to expand the love that my wife and I had for each other, and that feeling was solidified when I held my son in my arms for the first time. In that moment, I knew I would do anything for him and he did not have to do anything to earn that love.

What does this mean for unmarried people? Use the disciples as an example. If you are called to remain single (many people are), then find a community that you can unite with. Don't simply hope that you will stumble on a group like this. Make finding a community or building a community a top priority in your life. You were not created to be alone.

That is why I much prefer to call people who are not married "unmarried" rather than "single." I hate that we use the word "single" to refer to people who aren't married. When done well, these communities live in total transparency with each other. There are no secrets or divisions. Don't be single. If you're not called to marriage, don't allow yourself to get lonely. If you haven't found your community yet, keep searching.

It is not good for people to be alone.

Reflect: Do you have a relationship with someone who knows everything about you?

8

Resist Temptation

Accompanying Scripture Reading: Matthew 4:1-11

IN THE VERY BEGINNING of the Bible, we are introduced to the primary adversary of history. In the garden, this adversary took on the form of a serpent, but he was not given a name. In fact, throughout the Bible, the authors work hard to not give the satan a name. They did not want to give him that much respect. When we give someone a name, we give them dignity. Biblically speaking, naming a child is an act of love. In fact, naming someone is a spiritual act.

When the authors wrote about the satan, they used metaphors and descriptions of him. The most common description used is "the satan," which means "adversary." Eventually readers and translators grew uncomfortable with the cumbersome practice of talking about a character without a name and turned Scripture's description of the satan into his name, but the satan does not have a name. Every time the authors talk about the satan they use an article, "the," before the descriptor. They chose to call him "the satan" or "the devil."

Another name translators give the adversary is "Lucifer," but that word is simply the Latin name for Venus. Isaiah calls the satan "the morning star," another description of Venus because Venus is the last star we see before daylight. It is the star that rebels against the sun.

"Devil" is simply the Greek word for "slanderer," and the translators turned "devil" into another name for the satan by choosing not to translate it from the original Greek. There are times when the translators choose to translate the Greek word, but they do this when it is referring to someone other than the satan. It's the word Paul uses when he tells us not to gossip. In other words, we can be devils too.

The same is true with the word "satan." We are all satans (adversaries) at times. Even God is a "satan" when he opposes evil. However, "the" satan is not only "a" satan. He's "the satan," the primary villain, the opposer of goodness, but the power of this primary opposer has been greatly diminished. The good news is the satan has been bound. Unless God allows it, the satan can't hurt you. If you are God's child, the satan has no power over you. The only way he can hurt you is by convincing you to hurt yourself.

> [Jesus] disarmed the spiritual rulers and authorities. He shamed them publicly by his victory over them on the cross. (Col 2:15)

Christ is on the throne of his kingdom and we are the citizens of his kingdom. God's got us. The apostle Peter did say that the enemy is on a mission to destroy us, but we are assured that the enemy will fail.

> [The devil] prowls around like a roaring lion, looking for someone to devour. (1 Pet 5:8)

The satan wants to devour but he can't unless you help him. Although he can tempt you, the satan can't physically do anything to you, and Peter is speaking from experience here. When Peter tempted Jesus to not do what Jesus came to earth to do, Jesus called Peter a satan. Jesus told his disciples that he was going to die for them, and Peter tempted Jesus to not go through with it.

> Jesus turned to Peter and said, "Get away from me, Satan! You are a dangerous trap to me." (Matt 16:23)

Resist Temptation

When we sin, or when we tempt others to sin, we are a satan. Adam and Eve did it first and we keep the tradition going. All pain is caused by sin. Some of our pain is caused by our sin and some of it is caused by Adam's sin. So, how can we decrease pain in the world? Resist sin. Resist the satan.

> We are not fighting against flesh-and-blood enemies, but against evil rulers and authorities of the unseen world, against mighty powers in this dark world, and against evil spirits in the heavenly places. (Eph 6:12)

We are constantly being tempted, and one of the most common temptations is to believe we should fight for wealth, fame, or power. These are temptations that the devil threw at Jesus in the wilderness, but Jesus resisted. In fact, this is a temptation that was thrown at Jesus many times, but he never got distracted by wealth or politics. Jesus fought real evil.

After Jesus was baptized by John, he chose to begin his public ministry by fighting the devil. The fight was going to happen eventually, and he chose to set the tone for the war:

> Jesus was led by the Spirit into the wilderness to be tempted by the devil. After fasting forty days and forty nights, he was hungry. The tempter came to him and said, "If you are the Son of God, tell these stones to become bread." (Matt 4:1–3)

Many of us can relate to the satan's use of food and drink to tempt, but Jesus resisted. The satan went on to tempt Jesus with power and wealth, but Jesus resisted this temptation the same way he resisted every temptation, by quoting Scripture.

What could the satan do to Jesus in the wilderness? He tempted Jesus. That's all he can do, but if he can tempt Jesus, he can tempt us. Before God made us, the satan couldn't do anything but complain. Then people were created, and what did he have to do in the garden? He had to convince Eve to do the evil.

Genesis describes the satan as "shrewd." The original Hebrew word for "shrewd" is *arum*. That same word is used throughout Proverbs as a positive trait. It means clever or perceptive. In other words, he's very smart:

> The serpent was the shrewdest of all the wild animals the Lord God had made. One day he asked the woman, "Did God really say you must not eat the fruit from any of the trees in the garden?" "Of course we may eat fruit from the trees in the garden," the woman replied. "It's only the fruit from the tree in the middle of the garden

> that we are not allowed to eat. God said, 'You must not eat it or even touch it; if you do, you will die.'" "You won't die!" the serpent replied to the woman. "God knows that your eyes will be opened as soon as you eat it, and you will be like God, knowing both good and evil." The woman was convinced. (Gen 3:1–6)

It is obvious to me that the satan knew exactly with what to tempt Eve because, from an outsider's perspective, it seems Eve should have easily seen through the snake's lies. It appears that Eve wanted to eat the apple. She was curious.

We should fight the satan like Jesus, not like Adam and Eve, but if we're honest, most of us are more like Adam and Eve than we are like Jesus. There's a lot of enticing temptation in this world. To get us to sin, the satan usually just has to mention the things we want. We think that if he tempts us, we can blame him. We say, "the devil made me do it."

We elevate the satan and give him the dignity of a name because we want to be able to blame him. We want to believe he can control us so that we can blame him when we sin, but the good news is better than we give it credit for:

> Resist the devil, and he will flee from you. Come close to God, and God will come close to you. Wash your hands, you sinners. Purify your hearts, for your loyalty is divided between God and the world. (Jas 4:7–8)

What does this passage teach us to do to resist the satan?

1. Run to God.

You know what tempts you. Run from it and to God. Submit to God and his instructions and good things will happen. Fill your life with God, with his church. We think of "come close to God" as an emotional thing but it's very practical. Do what's right. Have a pure heart. Follow him and he will come close to you.

2. Humble yourself before God.

If we want to live the good life he calls us to, we must take sin seriously. Sin is incredibly harmful. It's sin because it hurts people. It's sin because it's bad for us. God loves us too much to condone harmful actions. I regularly tell my sons, "I love you too much to let you disobey."

We can't change the world if we live like the world. We have been recruited by God to a Christian mission, not a Sunday morning religion.

We are called to change the world, to be counter-cultural, but we can't do that if we just do what comes naturally.

3. Trust God's word.

Like Jesus did, we have God's word to fend off the attacks of the satan. How much of God's word do you know? How much do you intimately know?

> I have hidden your word in my heart, that I might not sin against you. (Ps 119:11)

It's not a list of dos and don'ts. It's a love letter from a father to his kids, and that letter gives wisdom because the author cares for his children. Resist the devil. Run to God and trust his word.

Reflect: Do you live counter-culturally, or do your actions look too much like the world's?

9

Fight Your Devils

Accompanying Scripture Reading: Luke 4:1–14

IN HIS TIME ON earth, Jesus regularly encountered evil spirits and he came out on top every time. So, what can we learn about how to combat evil spirits by studying the actions of Jesus? Luke 4:1–17 tells us the story of Jesus' temptation in the wilderness. Immediately after Jesus was baptized, the Holy Spirit led him to the wilderness where the devil attacked him. Jesus faced forty days of temptation by the devil, fasting all the while and feeling the pangs of hunger. The devil urged Jesus to turn a stone into bread. Jesus, anchored in Scripture, resisted, affirming that life transcends mere sustenance. The devil then showed him all the world's kingdoms, offering Jesus dominion in exchange for worship, but Jesus again appealed to Scripture, declaring sole allegiance to God. The devil then took Jesus to Jerusalem's pinnacle, urging a daring leap, citing angelic protection. Jesus rejected this test, emphasizing unwavering trust in God. Frustrated, the devil withdrew, biding time for the next opportune moment.

Jesus responded to the temptations of the devil with Scripture and so should we. Respond to the satan's attacks with the truth of Scripture.

Christians dominate the science of archeology because their confidence in the accuracy of the Bible leads them to prove its reliability. Over time, dust and debris accumulate on the ground, but by digging beneath that accumulation, archeologists can uncover history. For hundreds of years the discoveries made by archeologists have proven the accuracy of the Bible. In fact, there has never been a single archeological discovery that has disproven or contradicted the claims of the Bible. If historians or scientists ever make a discovery that contradicts a biblical claim, just wait. Their discoveries will someday be disproven.

Perhaps the most beneficial archeological discovery of our lifetime was the discovery of the Dead Sea Scrolls.[1] These scrolls were discovered in the 1940s, and they are two thousand years old. They are one thousand years older than the oldest biblical manuscripts we had before their discovery. You would assume that in that thousand-year period selfish, power-hungry, or flawed copiers would have changed details in the Bible, but that is not the case. The Dead Sea Scrolls confirmed the accuracy of the Bible. They also confirmed that the Bible is not only true but it is alive. There's nothing else like the Bible. Nothing comes close. So, trust it. Memorize it. Use it.

There's another story of an encounter with a devil in Luke 4:31–44. In this story, Jesus does more than use the word, he shows that he is the Word. In a Galilean town called Capernaum, Jesus often taught in the synagogue where he regularly left the locals astounded by his teaching. On one occasion, a man possessed by an evil spirit shouted when he recognized Jesus. Undeterred by the demonic outburst, Jesus rebuked the spirit, commanding its silence and expulsion from the afflicted man. To the astonishment of the onlookers, the demon convulsed the man before exiting, leaving him unharmed. The eyewitnesses marveled at the authority displayed in Jesus' words, acknowledging even the obedience of evil spirits to his command.

Why did Jesus encounter so many devils while it seems we so rarely come in contact with them? I see two reasons:

1. The fact that we don't recognize evil spirits doesn't mean they don't exist.

---

1. Zuckerman, "Dead Sea Scrolls."

We find what we look for. Jesus tells us to watch out for evil spirits. If we're not watching for evil spirits, we won't recognize them when they attack.

> For we are not fighting against flesh-and-blood enemies, but against evil rulers and authorities of the unseen world, against mighty powers in this dark world, and against evil spirits in the heavenly places. (Eph 6:12)

If you watch, you will likely see evidence of the spiritual world's impact on the physical world. Even if you have not found evil spirits, if you are a child of God, you have found something much more important. God tells us that if we will look for him, we will find him:

> If you look for me wholeheartedly, you will find me. (Jer 29:13)

Throughout history, people have convinced themselves gods are real, that coincidences were miracles, and that common sense was a god talking. They found gods everywhere, but not today. That's not what people search for. Today, most people are naturalists.

Most people don't invite demon possession like first-century supernaturalists did. I'm guessing not many of us have used a Ouija board lately, but even those who have probably did it skeptically. You saw it as a superstition or simply cardboard and plastic. However, the truth is that opening yourself up to unknown supernatural things can be extremely dangerous. That habit was common in Jesus' time and it led to a lot of demon possession.

Unfortunately, we primarily struggle with a different issue today. We see ourselves as "enlightened." Naturalists are most tempted to worship themselves. As a result, our demons are usually physical. They don't open us up to demon possession like worshiping other gods does. Instead, they keep us from searching for God at all.

A second reason we encounter evil spirits less often is a good one:

2. The growth of Christianity has hindered the satan's ability to freely attack.

If we believe the Holy Spirit lives in us, we are his temple. God's presence goes with us, and as we spread, he spreads. What does that mean for evil spirits? They're running out of room. There are fewer places for them to hide:

> The light shines in the darkness, and the darkness can never extinguish it. (John 1:5)

The Holy Spirit extinguishes darkness and darkness can't fight back. It's hopeless against God's light. If we are children of the light, if his unlimited power lives in us, we can never think of ourselves as victims. If you're a Christian, you're not a victim. You are a victor:

> The Spirit who lives in you is greater than the spirit who lives in the world. (1 John 4:4)

When you face your devils, you've been given every weapon you need to turn the battlefield into a mission field. Jesus turned his wilderness experience into a testimony of the power of God's word. Let God use your story for his glory.

Reflect: What are your most effective weapons in fighting evil spirits?

10

Follow Me

Accompanying Scripture Reading: Luke 5:1–11

HAVE YOU EVER FELT like you needed to change in order to fit into a group? I remember one morning recently when I went golfing with my brother who was a member of a country club. When I got to the venue, my brother took one look at what I was wearing and immediately said, "That won't work." I looked down at what I had on, a golf polo and some shorts that were made to look like cutoff pants. While I have definitely made some bad fashion choices before, getting rejected because of them was a new experience for me. My brother made it clear that to play golf at this country club, like most country clubs, you had to meet their fashion standards.

The church often falls into this trap. When we do not fight the temptation, we judge people who are not like us. We expect people to be like us before they can follow Jesus. That's religion. Religion says, "Change, then you can follow God," but Jesus said, "Follow me, then I will change you." It doesn't happen overnight, but if you follow Jesus, he will change you, usually through a gradual process.

Many of us get frustrated when we don't feel like we're making progress. Everyone who's ever been on a diet can relate to that feeling. However, the reason we don't feel like we're making progress is because it's happening gradually. Unfortunately, when we are religiously motivated, we see people come as they are; then we feel frustrated when they change slowly.

Jesus never put mile markers on our goodness, and in this life, there is not a spiritual maturity finish line. When it comes to spiritual maturity, we are always on a journey toward glorification. Glorification is the moment at which we are brought into heaven; until then, we continue to grow. Our goal is to be like Jesus, which is an impossible goal in this life. Therefore, the mandate is not "be good enough." The mandate is "follow me."

God doesn't give Christians a map. He gives them a driver's license. We do not have a step-by-step description of where we are going. Instead, we have an invitation to go.

Do you remember MapQuest? When I was in college, we used to print out a turn-by-turn description of our vacations. If we took even one wrong turn, we were lost. That is the problem with that kind of instruction: one wrong turn sabotages the plan. Driving without a map requires us to learn the roads. Through trial and error, and by asking for guidance, we learn.

Did you play Follow the Leader as a kid? In Follow the Leader, first a leader or "head of the line" is chosen. Then, the children line up behind the leader. The leader then moves around and all the children mimic the leader's actions. Any player who fails to follow is out of the game. The only way to lose a game of Follow the Leader is to stop following. That's what Christians do. We follow. We listen and obey.

The Bible contains four books that are biographies of Jesus' life: Matthew, Mark, Luke, and John. These four books are called the Gospels. Two of the books, Matthew and Luke, tell the story of Simon Peter's salvation:

> One day as Jesus was walking along the shore of the Sea of Galilee, he saw two brothers—Simon, also called Peter, and Andrew—throwing a net into the water, for they fished for a living. Jesus called out to them, "Come, follow me, and I will show you how to fish for people!" A little farther up the shore he saw two other brothers, James and John, sitting in a boat with their father, Zebedee, repairing their nets. And he called them to come, too. They

immediately followed him, leaving the boat and their father behind. (Matt 4:18–22)

Peter's decision to follow Jesus and abandon the family business would be seen by most people as irresponsible. As a child, I was always terrified by this story. I didn't want to have to leave my family to follow Jesus, but I was comforted when I read Luke's version of this story. Matthew tells the story, but he doesn't tell the whole story. That is likely because Matthew was writing to Jews, to people who had already decided to give their lives to religion. For them, it wasn't surprising to hear a story of people who dropped everything to follow a rabbi. But Luke was telling the story to gentiles. A gentile is anyone who is not Jewish, and that might be why Luke gave more information about the decision process.

Here's the beginning of Luke's version of the story:

> One day as Jesus was preaching on the shore of the Sea of Galilee, great crowds pressed in on him to listen to the word of God. He noticed two empty boats at the water's edge, for the fishermen had left them and were washing their nets. Stepping into one of the boats, Jesus asked Simon, its owner, to push it out into the water. So he sat in the boat and taught the crowds from there. (Luke 5:1–3)

Matthew left out the detail that Jesus was preaching. In fact, he preached so well the crowd pressed in on him, pushing him back into the water. That's important because Jesus' ministry was centered on his teaching, not on blind faith. Following Jesus begins with information. If anyone ever asks you to stop asking questions and just believe, don't follow them! They're trying to pull a fast one on you.

Peter was taking the beer cans and milk jugs out of his fishing nets. He was tired after fishing all night when Jesus asked Peter if he could use his boat as a stage. Peter had likely heard about Jesus before this, and maybe even seen him, but it seems that this was his first personal interaction with Jesus. Apparently, something Jesus said sparked some curiosity in Peter because he said yes, but the story didn't end with information. Jesus then performed a miracle and Peter was humbled. He fell to his knees and confessed his sinfulness. When Peter followed Jesus, he became aware of things about himself that needed to change. However, rather than rebuke Peter, Jesus comforted him. Peter was changed because he followed Jesus.

Think about what hung in the balance when Jesus invited Peter to "follow me." Imagine what hangs in the balance in your life as Jesus calls out, "Follow me!" Choosing to follow Jesus is the most important decision you will never make.

Reflect: Where has following Jesus led you that you wouldn't have gone on your own?

11

God Will Make You

Accompanying Scripture Reading: Matthew 4:12–22

OUR WORLD LOVES LEADERSHIP. It's all the rage. We have been trained to relentlessly pursue leadership and the power and wealth that it brings.

If you are a Christian, one thing is blatantly clear: followership is greater than leadership. Scripture says much more about how to follow than it does about how to lead. When the Bible does discuss leadership, it details who should not lead and it demonstrates how leaders should serve. The biblical model of leadership is followership.

Leadership corrupts. The only way to be a leader without being corrupted by it is to learn to be a servant leader and to put others before yourself. Our hearts are corrupt and we must take steps to reverse that corruption.

A few months ago, my six-year-old son said to my mom (who lives with us), "Grandma... if you don't tell my dad when I'm bad, I'll take care of you when you're old." Who taught this kid how to be evil?! No one. That comes naturally. No one has to teach a child to sin.

So, as sinful people, what do we need to do to avoid the urge to sin? We need to follow a leader who can teach us to do what is right. Most of us learn this lesson from our parents. We follow our parents and, if they're good parents, we learn and mature.

Our perfect Heavenly Father has promised to lead us in this maturing process. If we follow him, he will change us. What did Jesus say when he invited his disciples to follow him?

> Follow me, and I will make you fishers of men. (Matt 4:19 KJV)

It wouldn't make sense to go up to some fishermen and ask them to lead the Christian movement. They needed to follow first. This verse demonstrates that:

1. Following requires movement.

The disciples had to leave fishing nets, tax collector booths, and their families to follow Jesus. To mature, something in their life had to change. They had to move. To become the person God created you to be, you will have to leave your agenda and follow God's agenda for your life. You can't become like Christ and stay the same.

2. God does the making.

Emphasizing the truth that it is God who sanctifies us reminds us that we are powerless to do it alone. You're not going to grow by trying harder. The way to change yourself is to focus on Jesus. It's not about our behavior. It's about faith, about fully giving ourselves to the Christian agenda.

The story of the sinful woman who anointed Jesus' feet with perfume perfectly illustrates this point. One day, Jesus was invited to eat dinner at a Pharisee's house. As Jesus reclined at the table, a woman who was known in the city for her sinful past heard about the gathering. Undeterred by judgment, she entered with a precious alabaster jar filled with expensive perfume. Overwhelmed with emotion, she knelt behind Jesus, tears streaming down her face. With deep reverence, she wiped his feet with her hair, kissed them incessantly, and anointed them with the costly perfume. Given the woman's reputation, Simon the Pharisee silently questioned Jesus' prophethood, but Jesus responded to Simon's unspoken thoughts with a parable:

> Then Jesus told him this story: "A man loaned money to two people—500 pieces of silver to one and 50 pieces to the other. But neither of them could repay him, so he kindly forgave them both, canceling their debts. Who do you suppose loved him more after that?" Simon answered, "I suppose the one for whom he canceled the larger debt." "That's right," Jesus said. (Luke 7:41–43)

Redirecting attention to the woman, Jesus highlighted Simon's oversights. While Simon complained, the woman had lavished care on Jesus' feet. Jesus declared her sins forgiven, sparking murmurs among the men at the table, and, with a final assurance, Jesus spoke directly to the woman:

> I tell you, her sins—and they are many—have been forgiven, so she has shown me much love. But a person who is forgiven little shows only little love. (Luke 7:47)

The woman knew that she was a sinner and submitted to Christ. It is the recognition of dependence on God that allows us to be sanctified by him. Many people will say they believe in Jesus but will never actually follow him. The Pharisees respected Jesus enough to invite him to dinner, but their pride kept them from surrendering to his teaching. That's the story of Judas. He was drawn to Jesus, but he chose not to adopt Jesus' agenda for his life.

This is also the story of the Israelites all throughout Scripture. They were God's chosen people. He gave them a beautiful plan to live in harmony with him forever, but they chose to go their own way, to worship false gods, and to indulge in sinful behavior. This is also our story: Jesus died so that we can live in harmony with him, but so often we give in to the temptations of this world even though they lead to pain and division.

> May God himself, the God of peace, sanctify you through and through. May your whole spirit, soul and body be kept blameless at the coming of our Lord Jesus Christ. God will make this happen, for he who calls you is faithful. (1 Thess 5:23–24)

John Wesley taught that salvation includes two gifts of grace: justification and sanctification. That is a concept that is worth reflecting on. When we call ourselves Christians but don't become disciples of Jesus Christ by following him, we accept the first gift of grace (justification) and reject the second gift of grace (sanctification). We accept the justification that comes when our sins are forgiven, but we reject the sanctification that would make us the people God created us to be. When we reject sanctification, we become impotent Christians. However, when we allow the Holy Spirit to sanctify us, we become people who are more obedient to him and more useful to him. Don't accept justification and reject the Holy Spirit's sanctification.

Reflect: Is there anything holding you back from fully surrendering to God's work of sanctification in your life?

12

Don't Forget to Feast

Accompanying Scripture Reading: John 2:1–12

Jesus healed many people, but his first miracle didn't heal anyone. For his first miracle, he turned water into wine. Why was this his first miracle? I believe it was for two reasons:

1. Jesus turned water into wine to honor his mother.

   > Honor your father and mother. Then you will live a long, full life in the land the Lord your God is giving you. (Exod 20:12)

   Because of the promise given at the end of the fifth commandment, I've always believed that honoring our parents leads to blessings. I used to beg my parents to give me advice so I could follow it. I wanted their blessing and I wanted the blessing that would come from following their advice.

2. Jesus turned water into wine to keep the party going.

In Jesus' day, scheduled celebrations were at the heart of Jewish culture, and wedding celebrations went on for a week. Once, Jesus attended a wedding in Cana with his mother, Mary, and his recently recruited disciples. During the celebration, the hosts ran out of wine. Mary, noticing the issue, asked Jesus to make more wine for them, and Jesus resisted. He replied,

> "My time has not yet come." (John 2:4)

Nonetheless, Mary ignored Jesus' objections and instructed the servants to obey Jesus' instructions. Nearby stood six stone water jars, each holding twenty to thirty gallons, used for Jewish ceremonial washing. Jesus told the servants to fill the jars with water and they filled them to the brim. Then he told them to dip some out and take it to the master of ceremonies. The servants followed his instructions and when the master of ceremonies tasted the water that had been turned into wine, he celebrated and complimented the wine:

> "A host always serves the best wine first," [the master of ceremonies] said. "Then, when everyone has had a lot to drink, he brings out the less expensive wine. But you have kept the best until now!" (John 2:10)

This miraculous event was the first of the signs Jesus performed. It revealed his glory, and his disciples believed in him.

This passage tells us Jesus made 180 gallons of wine! That's 900 bottles of wine . . . on the wall. Perhaps Jesus was preparing them for heaven. We know very little about what heaven will be like, but we do know one thing we will do in heaven: feast. We are going to party, and that should not be surprising to us. When God gives his people instructions, he usually includes the importance of holidays (holy days). When God established the old covenant with the Jews, he told them to celebrate seven festivals every year.

King David also loved to party:

> [God] makes grass grow for the cattle, and plants for people to cultivate—bringing forth food from the earth: wine that gladdens human hearts, oil to make their faces shine, and bread that sustains their hearts. (Ps 104:14–15 NIV)

It seems that he wants us to be happy, hot, and healthy. David is painting a picture of paradise. He's taking us back to Adam's garden where we had everything we needed. God makes some things for enjoyment. He gives us wine to make us happy.

There are, however, some biblical cautions about partying. How should we enjoy wine? Let's go back to Adam's garden for some context. God placed two kinds of trees in Adam's garden:

1. Some trees are for food.

One of the trees in the center of the garden was the Tree of Life. That tree was meant to provide food. It could have sustained Adam and Eve forever, but there was a second tree in the middle of the garden. It was the Tree of Knowledge of Good and Evil. That tree was not meant for food.

2. Some trees are for enjoyment or beauty.

They were invited to enjoy its beauty but not to eat its fruit. Too often with alcohol, we've mixed the purposes. When we drink it as if it is food instead of sipping it to enjoy its beauty, we misuse it. So, let's discuss how we should use alcohol.

How do we wisely enjoy the beauty of wine?

1. Be careful how you drink.

Some drinking habits and some drinks are designed purely to get people drunk. Avoid those:

> Don't be drunk with wine, because that will ruin your life. (Eph 5:18)

You can enjoy it, but don't misuse it. If you misuse it, you'll turn glad hearts into sad hearts, like Adam did with the fruit.

2. Be careful where you drink.

Do not drink around someone who is tempted to misuse alcohol. If your drinking tempts someone else to get drunk, don't drink:

> If what I eat causes another believer to sin, I will never eat meat again as long as I live—for I don't want to cause another believer to stumble. (1 Cor 8:13)

If you've ever been addicted, run from whatever it is that you have been addicted to.

In addition, don't drink alone. If wine was intended to help us celebrate the good things that God has done, it should be an act of fellowship, and good community can help us drink responsibly. God gave us wine to remember, not to forget.

3. Be careful why you drink.

This will likely disqualify a lot of drinking habits. Don't use drinking as an escape. It doesn't work. It will not help you escape your problem. In fact, if you attempt to use it for that purpose, it will only make your problems worse:

> Who has anguish? Who has sorrow? Who is always fighting? Who is always complaining? Who has unnecessary bruises? Who has bloodshot eyes? It is the one who spends long hours in the taverns, trying out new drinks. (Prov 23:29–30)

If you turn to alcohol to cover your pain, you're just causing more pain. Instead, when we struggle, we turn to God:

> Jesus said, "Come to me, all of you who are weary and carry heavy burdens, and I will give you rest." (Matt 11:28)

The master of ceremonies at the wedding ceremony in John 2 pointed out that hosts bring out the cheap wine when people are drunk. In other words, drinking makes you dumber. That also means we would be wise to avoid making decisions when we drink.

The master of ceremonies also pointed out that Jesus' wine was the best wine. If Jesus' opening miracle was intended to make people happy, why is the church so tempted by heavy-handed justice and anger? Christians are called to live joyfully under God's grace.

Jesus' introduction of the kingdom is a feast! It's fun! The wedding in Cana is a glimpse of the new kingdom, the new heaven and the new earth. It's time for Christians to learn how to enjoy and celebrate life:

> People should eat and drink and enjoy the fruits of their labor, for these are gifts from God. (Eccl 3:13)

Yes, gifts should be enjoyed responsibly, but they should be enjoyed. Your life is a gift!

When God put Adam and Eve in the garden, he announced his first command: eat freely (Gen 2:16). Then, in the book of Revelation, God gave his last command: drink freely (Rev 22:17), but that invitation is to drink the water of life.

Don't forget to feast, to celebrate together the great things that God has done.

Reflect: Are you good at celebrating the good things God has accomplished in your life?

13

God Blesses Hurting People

Accompanying Scripture Reading: Matthew 5:1–16

Jesus spent most of his time with tax collectors, zealots, prostitutes, beggars, and outcasts. When you read the story of Jesus in the Gospels, you read about regular interactions with the lonely, the least, and the lost. When he talks to political elites, he rebukes them. When he talks to sinners, he heals them:

> Tax collectors and other notorious sinners often came to listen to Jesus teach. This made the Pharisees and teachers of religious law complain that he was associating with such sinful people—even eating with them! (Luke 15:1–2)

The most famous sermon Jesus ever preached is called the Sermon on the Mount. It begins in Matt 5. He gathered a huge crowd and told them about his upside-down kingdom. To preach this sermon, Jesus sat down on a hill with his disciples and talked about people who are blessed, but the list of people he gave was a list of people who are traditionally pitied or rejected by society. The poor in spirit are blessed because they recognize their need for God. People who mourn are blessed because God will comfort them. Meek people are blessed for their humility. People who hunger and thirst for righteousness will be blessed for their desire to live according to God's will. Merciful people are blessed because they demonstrate compassion and forgiveness. People who are pure in heart are blessed because of their sincere intentions. Peacemakers are blessed and called children of God, and people who are persecuted are blessed and are promised the kingdom of heaven.

Their culture would have said God blesses the wealthy and well-connected, the powerful and influential, but Jesus said God blesses outsiders. He's not saying he won't bless insiders, but they are statistically less likely to receive his blessing.

Imagine this: you order a pizza and the delivery guy shows up holding the pizza in his hands with no box. There's cheese oozing down his arm. What would you think? You would wonder where his hands have been. You would ask him, "Where's the box?" He'd reply, "You just ordered the pizza, not a box." You'd be furious. Why? Because when you order a pizza, you expect the pizza to come in a vessel. When you're hungry, you don't think, "I'm going to buy a box." The box without a pizza has no value. What am I going to do with an empty box? Throw it away. Not long ago I walked into an Old Chicago Pizza and asked them for a box. They just gave it to me, for free. It probably costs them fifty cents. That's nothing to them. So what makes the box valuable? The box becomes valuable when there is a pizza in it. A vessel becomes valuable when its contents are valuable.

We are like pizza boxes, and we live in a world of people who love to brag about how pretty their box is. People determine their worth by their appearance, but their boxes are empty. Comparing the beauty of one pizza box to another is pointless. When I order pizza, I want to know how good the pizza in the box is, not how pretty the box is. In fact, my favorite pizza comes from a restaurant with plain white boxes.

Our beauty, wealth, power, or popularity on Instagram mean nothing if we are empty. Someday, our bodies will die, and without God, our bodies are worthless. However, if God is in you, your value cannot be measured. If God is in you, you are infinitely valuable. Christians are vessels who choose to surrender their agendas to be used by God.

Elisha was a prophet of God to the nation of Israel and in 2 Kgs 4:1–7, when one of his disciples died, the disciple's widow came to ask Elisha for help. When her husband died his creditors came to take his sons into slavery because that is how their culture handled debt. Elisha, moved by her plight, asked her about her possessions. She lamented having nothing substantial except for a small amount of oil. Elisha, determined to offer a solution, instructed her to borrow jugs and bowls from her neighbors. Once gathered, she was to lock herself and her sons in their home, pouring oil into each container until they were all filled. Following Elisha's guidance, she collected as many containers as she could find. As she poured the oil, it miraculously kept flowing until every vessel was full and, when the last container was filled, the oil ceased. Recognizing the miracle, she reported the extraordinary event to Elisha. In response, Elisha advised her to sell the oil, settle her debts, and use the remaining funds to provide for herself and her sons. Grateful for the guidance, she embarked on a journey to turn the surplus oil into a source of financial relief and security for her family.

Notice that when the vessels were being filled, they didn't care what the vessels looked like. They just wanted more vessels. The vessels became valuable when they were filled with oil.

In those days, oil was often used as fuel for fire. It was their light. Throughout Scripture, oil represents the presence of the Holy Spirit. When someone is anointed with oil, it is meant to signify they are filled with the Holy Spirit.

For a pizza box to be useful it must be clean and empty.

1. Clean

The box can't clean itself. Someone else must do this for it. You can't clean yourself, but Jesus has offered to do that for you.

2. Empty

If the pizza box is full of junk, there is no room for pizza. If we are full of ourselves, full of self-sufficiency, pride, anger, and skepticism, there is no room in our life for God.

Jesus prioritized ministry to the least of these because they were empty vessels. The pretty vessels filled themselves with worthless junk. There was no room for Jesus in them, so he went to the ugly vessels. You will never be pretty enough, strong enough, rich enough, or famous enough to experience

THE LIFE

true fulfillment, because it is not you who makes you valuable. The only way to experience true fulfillment is to allow God to make you valuable.

Reflect: Which is more likely to get in the way of God using you: pride or self-doubt?

14

Breaking the Chains of Father Wounds

Accompanying Scripture Reading: Matthew 5:38–48

IN JESUS' SERMON ON the Mount, there is a theme of forgiveness and generosity that seems almost naïve. To internalize this teaching, we need to reflect on one of the hardest people to forgive, our fathers. Fathers inevitably cause wounds because no father is perfect. These wounds, also known as daddy issues or father complexes, permeate us deeply. While some might carry deeper scars, the truth remains: our relationship with our father has a profound impact on us.

> Direct your children onto the right path, and when they are older,
> they will not leave it. (Prov 22:6)

The first step in directing your children onto the right path is knowing the path. Too many fathers fail to direct their children because they have not learned what the right path is.

When my generation thinks of good fathers, we think of Danny Tanner, Carl Winslow, Philip Banks, Tim Taylor, and Bill Cosby . . . too soon? Unfortunately, none of these fathers fulfill the commandment to direct their children onto the right path because the right path is the path to God. It doesn't matter that their advice made us feel good, because the path to God must be the top priority and main objective:

> You can enter God's Kingdom only through the narrow gate. The highway to hell is broad, and its gate is wide for the many who choose that way. But the gateway to life is very narrow and the road is difficult, and only a few ever find it. (Matt 7:13–14)

Living in God's kingdom in this world means living the good life. The quality of our relationship with our father significantly influences our connection with God and therefore the health of our lives in this world. A father can have great intentions, but if they do not lead their children on the narrow path to God, that father will lead their children to destruction.

Only 2 percent of children whose dads don't go to church will become lifelong churchgoers, but 44 percent of kids become lifelong churchgoers if their dads regularly take them to church.[1] Statistically, the most important factor in the transmission of faith between generations is a healthy relationship with our fathers. This does not mean people with good dads are dumber and therefore more gullible when it comes to spirituality. It means that the wounds that are caused by an unhealthy relationship with your father can blind you to truth. Father wounds can eclipse our view of God, like the moon can block our view of the sun. The moon is smaller but it's closer.

In other words, people aren't leaving the faith because it's not true. They're leaving the faith because it doesn't feel good. Most people choose beliefs based on relationships in their communities. If people were leaving the faith because they discovered it wasn't true, it wouldn't have anything to do with relationships.

It is possible, however, to discover the right path without the direction of a quality Christian father, but those who do will walk that path with wounds created by their fathers.

We are not destined to repeat the mistakes of our fathers. Our fathers affect a lot about who we are, but if you had a bad dad, don't be a victim. Don't let it define you. You are more than your pain. Your Heavenly Father

---

1. Stonestreet and Morris, "Dads, Take Your Kids to Church!"

can rescue you when your earthly father hurt you. I will give you some proof.

When you look at the genealogy of Jesus Christ you will see that there are examples of good fathers that produced bad children, and there are bad dads that produced good children:

> Rehoboam was the father of Abijah. Abijah was the father of Asa. Asa was the father of Jehoshaphat. Jehoshaphat was the father of Jehoram. (Matt 1:7–8)

Rehoboam was a bad dad that begat a bad son. Abijah was a bad dad that begat a good son. Asa was a good dad that begat a good son, and Jehoshaphat was a good father that begat a bad son. What does this mean? You did not inherit your dad's unrighteousness. You can break the chain and be set free.

Let's discuss what causes a dad to be labeled a bad dad. There are many types of dads that produce a variety of father wounds. Here are some of them:

- Tyrannical Dad

The children of a tyrannical dad are never good enough for him. His expectations are so high that kids could never meet them. Sometimes these dads are angry or abusive. They might have great goals but many times their goals are selfish.

- Overbearing Dad

The overbearing dad is available to his kids. He attends PTA events and takes his kids on vacations. He chooses his kid's football game over watching a football game on TV, but sometimes he puts too much pressure on his kids. His desire for them to succeed can become overwhelming.

- Hollow Dad

The hollow dad might be around physically, but he is emotionally unavailable. He's so caught up in his work, his hobbies, or his problems that he doesn't take enough time to invest in his kids.

- In-and-Out Dad

The most common situation that causes a dad to be an in-and-out dad is divorce and shared custody. Sometimes these kids get too excited to see their dads because it doesn't happen often enough.

- Absent Dad

An absent dad is a dad that isn't available to his kids at all. This often happens when a dad leaves his family or dies early.

This is not an exhaustive list but it gives an idea of the types of actions that cause wounds. There is a profound link between your relationship with your father and your ability to sustain relationships, find contentment in work, parent effectively, and assert yourself in conversations. In other words, your relationship with your father significantly affects your ability to live a happy life. So, what can we do when we recognize our relationship with our father has negatively affected us?

A prophecy about Jesus predicted that he would unite children with their fathers:

> His preaching will turn the hearts of fathers to their children, and the hearts of children to their fathers. (Mal 4:6)

If you obey the instructions of Jesus, your father wounds can be healed. Here are four steps to heal father wounds found in the Sermon on the Mount:

1. Change your identity.

You are more than your dad's son or daughter. He may have made you miserable in the past, but that is your past. It's not who you are. You have a new life. You are a new creation. Remove your dad's power over you.

> God blesses those who work for peace, for they will be called the children of God. (Matt 5:9)

If God really is who he says he is, the King of kings and Lord of lords, and you are his child, then your relationship with your Heavenly Father is the most important thing about you.

2. Pray for your dad.

Depending on how deeply he wounded you, praying for your dad might be a difficult step, but Jesus says it is a necessary step:

> Love your enemies! Pray for those who persecute you! (Matt 5:44)

3. Build relationships.

Build a relationship with God first, then with others. You will need friends or family that you can rely on as you walk the painful road toward forgiveness.

4. Forgive your father.

Forgiveness isn't a shortcut. It's not something you do quickly to get it over with, but it's better than vengeance. Vengeance is not freedom. When you choose vengeance, you chain your future to the future of the person you hate. Forgiveness is the only way to free yourself from them:

> If you forgive those who sin against you, your heavenly Father will forgive you. But if you refuse to forgive others, your Father will not forgive your sins. (Matt 6:14–15)

We are set free when we forgive others, and we are set free when we are forgiven. Your father might not deserve forgiveness, but neither did we when Jesus forgave us:

> Oh, what joy for those whose disobedience is forgiven, whose sin is put out of sight! (Ps 32:1)

The best way I know to forgive someone is to seek to understand them. When you see them as broken, sinful people, you begin to see why they did what they did. This does not justify their actions but helps us to understand them. If your dad did terrible things to you, ask yourself why he did those things. Figure out what drove him to do it so that you can begin to see him as a broken human. Get to the point where you can pity him and rise above him:

> Never pay back evil with more evil. Do things in such a way that everyone can see you are honorable. Do all that you can to live in peace with everyone. Dear friends, never take revenge. Leave that to the righteous anger of God. For the Scriptures say, "I will take revenge; I will pay them back," says the Lord. Instead, "If your enemies are hungry, feed them. If they are thirsty, give them something to drink. In doing this, you will heap burning coals of shame on their heads." Don't let evil conquer you, but conquer evil by doing good. (Rom 12:17–21)

Reflect: Is your relationship with your earthly father more likely to cause you to doubt or to trust your Heavenly Father?

15

How to Pray

Accompanying Scripture Reading: Matthew 6:1–18

WHAT DOES YOUR PRAYER life look like? Have you scheduled a time for prayer every day?

The purpose of prayer is not to get things out of God. It's to build intimacy with God. If you start a conversation with God by asking him for a new truck, you might get a new truck. However, you would be revealing your misunderstanding of the purpose of a relationship with God. God does give us incredibly good gifts, but he does it to build intimacy with us. Also, if the gift you're asking for won't be good for you, he won't give it to you. He loves you too much to hurt you by giving you something that will eventually cause pain:

> The earnest prayer of a righteous person has great power and produces wonderful results. (Jas 5:16)

How to Pray

What are the wonderful results that prayer produces? It may seem that God supernaturally interacts with his children less often than he did in the past, but I don't believe that is the reality. The miracles we read about in Scripture might appear more frequent than they are because Scripture is a summary of thousands of years of God interacting with his creation. When God gave us free will, he chose not to perform miracles every time free will led to negative outcomes.

It is also possible we are less likely to see miracles because we have spent so much of our time making our lives comfortable and removing the need for God's help. It seems to me that God performs more miracles in places where people are desperate or where people have put their faith in him and not in themselves.

With that said, self-serving miracles aren't necessarily the wonderful result that James was talking about. The ultimate goal of prayer isn't health and wealth. The goal of prayer is a relationship with God. Communication is a primary key to healthy relationships and prayer is how we communicate with God.

Start your prayers with some relationship building statements: "Good morning, God. I love you, God." Then be honest with him: "God, I'm hurting right now," or "God, I'm so pumped right now." Having a regular prayer routine is the best way to build a personal relationship with God. Make a daily plan to pray and use prayer to build a greater relationship with God.

In the Sermon on the Mount, just before Jesus gave us the Lord's Prayer, Jesus told his followers not to pray in a flashy way to impress people. We don't need to ask God for things to inform him of our needs. He already knows everything we need and want. We ask God for things to build a relationship with him. Then, after some teaching about private prayer, Jesus taught us how to pray:

> Pray like this: Our Father in heaven, may your name be kept holy. May your Kingdom come soon. May your will be done on earth, as it is in heaven. Give us today the food we need, and forgive us our sins, as we have forgiven those who sin against us. And don't let us yield to temptation, but rescue us from the evil one. (Matt 6:9–13)

When we use Jesus' prayer as an outline, we start with worship and then pray that God's will is done. In the garden of Gethsemane, Jesus begged his Father to find a different way to save the world, but he then told his Father to do what his Father knew was right. Jesus asked his Father for something, and his Father rejected Jesus' request.

The Life

Continuing in the Lord's prayer, Jesus then asked that his needs would be provided for, and he asked for forgiveness. We know that Jesus was praying this prayer to teach his disciples how to pray, because Jesus never sinned. He had no need to ask for forgiveness. We are then taught to ask God for help in forgiving others, and we are to pray for safety and protection. When we pray this prayer, God hears us and responds in the best way possible.

Prayer is a conversation with God, and it should amaze us that the creator of the world wants to converse with and have a relationship with those whom he created. When we take for granted the amazing gift of prayer because we have had easy access to it for so long, we fail to experience the gratitude that prayer should produce. Prayer is an amazing gift from God who wants to be in a relationship with each of us.

> Always be joyful. Never stop praying. Be thankful in all circumstances, for this is God's will for you who belong to Christ Jesus. (1 Thess 5:16–18)

One day, Jesus was talking to his disciples, hoping to get them prepared for his inevitable departure from earth. He would no longer be with them physically, and he wanted to make sure they knew that his physical departure would not end their relationship:

> I am the true grapevine, and my Father is the gardener. He cuts off every branch of mine that doesn't produce fruit, and he prunes the branches that do bear fruit so they will produce even more. (John 15:1–2)

If we are a branch connected to Jesus, we will produce fruit that we can only produce if we are connected to Jesus. We will be people of love, joy, peace, patience, kindness, goodness, faithfulness, gentleness, and self-control:

> But if you remain in me and my words remain in you, you may ask for anything you want, and it will be granted! When you produce much fruit, you are my true disciples. This brings great glory to my Father. (John 15:7–8)

Jesus has a gift for you, abundant life. It's found as you grow more intentionally in your relationship with him. If you seriously want it, you will be willing to set up the habits that can assist you in finding it. God is going to love you no matter what, but if you choose to be more intentional in your prayer life, you will move one step closer to the blessed life. Find a quiet place. Turn off the notifications and spend time with Jesus.

Reflect: What are two specific times every day that you can set aside to talk to God?

16

Renewed by Grace

Accompanying Scripture Reading: Matthew 6:19–34

CHRISTIANS LOVE THE FACT that God is so close to us. However, it doesn't always feel like God is with us. Sometimes it feels like God is nowhere to be found.

All of us are like a bucket with a bunch of little holes in it. When we learn that God loves us unconditionally and that he will forgive us for sinning, our buckets are filled with gratitude, excitement, and passion. Unfortunately, our passion fades faster than we want it to. Our buckets leak.

A relationship with God is like other relationships. It's exciting in the beginning, but there are hard seasons. A relationship can start with a sizzle, but it will start to fizzle. When we are in the beginning of a romantic relationship, the honeymoon phase is often the best time. Have you ever noticed that things you used to think were cute about your partner aren't so cute anymore? When you were dating, you loved how she would hold her coffee with two hands and sip it. Now, after being married for two years, it drives you nuts. You say, "Stop slurping your coffee so loud!" So, what do you do? You invest in the relationship. You find ways to rekindle the excitement that was there in the beginning.

To keep our bucket full, we have to continually refill it. That's why we go to church to sing worship songs and hear good sermons. Some of us read inspirational books, pray, and worship God in nature. These things refill our bucket but the bucket continues to leak. If we stay connected to God, his grace fills us with everything we need to faithfully follow him, but the news gets even better. God's grace not only fills us, God's grace fills us and seals us.

The longer we are in relationship with God, the more the holes in our buckets are sealed. We learn biblical truth and gain confidence. We follow Christ's instructions and remove a bad habit. We set our eyes on Jesus and the temptations of this world are less distracting. We pray and get peace.

We call this process "sanctification." It is the process of becoming the people God created us to be, but it is usually a slow process. If you're reading this, you still have holes in your bucket. So, what do you do? Stay connected to God. Keep filling the bucket. Remind yourself of the incredible hope that we have in Jesus:

> And as God's grace reaches more and more people, there will be great thanksgiving, and God will receive more and more glory. That is why we never give up. Though our bodies are dying, our spirits are being renewed every day. (2 Cor 4:15-16)

What are the implications of the word "renewed" in this passage? It implies that hope fades. Passion wanes. And Paul says we're being renewed every day! Jesus tells us that if we will stay connected to him, he will refill our buckets with everything we need:

> Seek the Kingdom of God above all else, and live righteously, and he will give you everything you need. So don't worry about tomorrow, for tomorrow will bring its own worries. Today's trouble is enough for today. (Matt 6:33-34)

I'm writing this on a Tuesday and there are things I have to worry about today. Today has Tuesday trouble and tomorrow will bring Wednesday trouble. That's not me being a prophet. That's just life, but there's good news. There's a verse in Lamentations that I have relied on my whole life. I need it:

> The steadfast love of the Lord never ceases; his mercies never come to an end; they are new every morning; great is your faithfulness. (Lam 3:22–23)

Tomorrow has trouble coming but it also has grace coming. I was given grace this morning that was designed for today.

Let's go back to the 2 Corinthians passage. In it, Paul echoes Jesus:

> For our present troubles are small and won't last very long. Yet they produce for us a glory that vastly outweighs them and will last forever! So we don't look at the troubles we can see now; rather, we fix our gaze on things that cannot be seen. For the things we see now will soon be gone, but the things we cannot see will last forever. (2 Cor 4:17–18)

I recently read a story of a pastor who left his faith in Jesus because he got cancer, and I am amazed by the shortsightedness of his decision. If there is ever a time that he needs to refill his bucket, it's now. He needs the new mercies of Jesus today, but rather than look to Jesus for help, he is blaming Jesus. He is blaming Jesus for the pain that sin has caused.

Throughout history, people have made bad decisions (sin) that lead to pain, and those bad decisions had consequences for both the people who made the decisions and for the people around them. Bad decisions are like stacked dominos. When I knock over my domino, it will slam into the dominos of my wife and kids. Throughout history, consequences have compounded exponentially. The sins of Adam and Eve caused pain in the lives of their children and the dominos have tumbled all the way to us.

As Christians, it is our responsibility to end as much of the suffering as possible. As the holes in our buckets are sealed, we cause less pain for us and for others. However, until we are glorified, we recognize that the pain of this world is a result of our rebellion toward God, not a result of the actions of God.

So why doesn't God just make us all entirely sanctified right now? He could. In fact, someday he will. Someday he will make all his children perfect, but not yet. We beg, "God, just take away the temptation. Take the selfishness and make me generous. Take away the sadness and give me joy. Heal my body. Fulfill my desires." And he will do those things, but first we have lessons to learn and God has glory to get.

God's plan does not include an instantaneous end to sin and pain. That would require him to make me perfect. If God is going to get the glory, the hope of the world can't be my perfection. He is the hope of the world, not me. That's why God sanctifies us slowly. The fact that we run out of gas every day puts us in the station and that's where he wants us so we remember where the gas comes from. He wants us to set our eyes on him, not on our own perfection.

Allow Jesus to refill your bucket today. Trust his timing and thank him for continuing to fill the holes in your life.

Reflect: Which of your life habits would you have to change in order to create a routine of daily filling your soul with more of Jesus?

17

Don't Build Offense

Accompanying Scripture Reading: Matthew 7:1–6

ARE YOU EASILY ANNOYED? When I am in a bad mood, the smallest thing can set me off. When I am emotionally unhealthy, my response to the actions of others can be incredibly immature.

My wife has this habit of putting pills in her mouth then talking. I don't know why. It's like she waits until it's time to take her pills to start a conversation. It drives me crazy because I hate the idea of tasting pills. I swallow them as fast as I can. The other day I was irritable because my sons were not behaving and when my wife tried to tell me something with a mouth full of pills, I snapped. Apparently, I think I don't have any bad habits.

Those of you who are married, what is the thing you argue about most with your spouse? Most disagreements in relationships are never resolved. We just keep having them over and over. Why? Because most disagreements are based on pride. We think our way is better than their way. It could be something serious or it could be something like, "You never put your clothes away." "Close your mouth when you chew." "Stop biting your fingernails." "You're always late."

Jesus taught us to be patient with the flaws of others and focus on improving ourselves:

> Why worry about a speck in your friend's eye when you have a log in your own? How can you think of saying to your friend, "Let me help you get rid of that speck in your eye," when you can't see past the log in your own eye? Hypocrite! First get rid of the log in your own eye; then you will see well enough to deal with the speck in your friend's eye. (Matt 7:3–5)

Sometimes I think the reason the speck in my wife's eyes drives me crazy is because it's made of the same stuff as the log in my eye. Maybe I recognize the speck because I'm self-conscious about the log. My goal shouldn't be to get all the specks out of my wife's eye. We don't start a relationship with people to fix them. Christ teaches us how to serve our partners and our friends, to give more to them and expect less from them.

Pointing out little flaws in someone else is called nagging, and it's prideful. Eventually nagging turns into tension, then arguments, and ultimately division. If you are frustrated by how someone communicates, spends money, or spends time, you will either get over it or build a fence between you and them. This happens in marriage all the time. Offenses build fences.

How hard is it to communicate when there is a fence between you and the person with whom you're communicating? It's not easy. You can shout back and forth or just text each other, but that won't work for long. Eventually you'll start chucking grenades over the fence. If you spend too much time yelling at someone you're in a relationship with, find a way to remove the fence.

Thankfully, the Bible has a lot to say about how to make ourselves more like Christ in order to make our relationships better. Paul gave some advice to the Ephesians about how to treat each other, and I think it will help us to remove some of these offenses:

> Always be humble and gentle. Be patient with each other, making allowance for each other's faults because of your love. Make every effort to keep yourselves united in the Spirit, binding yourselves together with peace. (Eph 4:2–3)

If offenses are dividing your relationship, here are some steps to break the fences.

Step 1: Be humble.

This is the step where we take inventory of our strengths and weaknesses. For married couples, this is where we admit that we rely on the strengths of our spouse to balance our weaknesses and we allow our strengths to make up for our spouse's weakness. I'm guessing there aren't many perfect people reading this. So let's stop expecting our spouses to be good at everything. If it annoys you that your spouse isn't very organized, it could be because you've been given the ability to be organized. Let your strengths make up for their weaknesses, and don't let that frustrate you.

This is why I hate the way most Americans do weddings. We've turned it into an excuse to be selfish. We plan weddings with statements like, "Today is all about you." As a result, young couples start their married life with a pile of debt. It's a broken system. According to Scripture, when you get married you are signing up to sacrifice for someone else for the rest of your life. So why do we start it with a day that is all about getting everything we want? If you go into a marriage thinking about the things that a spouse will give you, you're setting yourself up for failure. If you want a healthy marriage, go into it thinking about the things that you can give to your spouse to make him or her a better person.

Step 2: Be gentle.

Gentleness isn't really in our nature because comfort brings confidence. We get really comfortable in our relationships and that confidence turns into forcefulness and bluntness. If you are in a relationship with someone long enough, you get comfortable and you say what's on your mind to people with whom you are comfortable. If you feel frustration, you vocalize frustration. As Christians, we are commanded to be gentle and slow to speak when we are frustrated.

Step 3: Be patient.

When Darci and I first moved to Wyoming, we traveled to Billings, Montana, for a weekend trip. We left Billings late at night because we couldn't afford a hotel room, so Darci agreed to drive for the first shift. Knowing that Darci is terrible with directions, I navigated to Gillette on my iPhone so all she would have to do is follow Siri's instructions. I quickly fell asleep, and, because Darci is so kind, she turned off the volume on the phone so it wouldn't wake me up. Unfortunately, that meant she could no longer hear Siri's instructions. For hours my phone, on silent, told Darci to turn south but she drove east. I woke up just in time to see a sign that said, "Welcome to North Dakota." For those of you who are directionally challenged, North Dakota is not between Billings, Montana, and Gillette, Wyoming.

If you are in a relationship with someone for any significant period of time, you will have many opportunities to demonstrate patience, and when we are patient, we create intimacy with the people to whom we show grace.

When I realize Darci has been doing something for me without telling me, I feel incredible gratitude. For me, there's no better motivator to give more to Darci than when I realize she has been doing things for me that should be my responsibility.

We don't realize the power our silence has. We underestimate the power of not sticking up for ourselves. I am not saying you should allow yourself to be abused, but in many cases you can make a larger impact if you don't point out that you are doing more than your fair share.

And on the other side of the coin, pay attention to the good things your spouse is doing and assume they are doing more than you know about. We tend to think we do more than we actually do and we think other people do less than they actually do. But even if they aren't carrying their share of the weight, we choose to make allowances for each other's faults.

Step 4: Be united.

When two people get married they become one person. The very nature of our creation shows that we were created to be united with people in a sacrificial way.

Later in Eph 4, Paul talks about bad relationship behaviors:

> Get rid of all bitterness, rage, anger, harsh words, and slander, as well as all types of evil behavior. Instead, be kind to each other,

> tenderhearted, forgiving one another, just as God through Christ has forgiven you. (Eph 4:31–32)

Most of this list has to do with how to react to being wronged. We often get bitter when something harmful is done to us, and to obey this command, we have to learn to forgive.

Step 5: Be free.

To be free we must forgive. Inability to forgive will hurt us much more than it will hurt the people we are mad at. Even when we think we deserve to be mad, forgiveness is the healthier option. It's a sacrificial act that requires us to be courageously unfair.

We also choose to be free of evil behavior. If there is something that has control of you, the best thing you can do is shine a light on it. Take intentional steps to remove temptation from your life. Do something that makes it harder to do those things you know you shouldn't do.

Step 6: Be kind.

We think of kindness in emotional terms, but kindness isn't an emotional action. Kindness, by definition, is a sacrificial action. You can be kind to someone even if you don't feel like it.

We are naturally good at critiquing and judging people. Christians, can we become the people with whom others want to be in relationship?

Reflect: Based on these descriptions, is it harder for you to be humble, gentle, patient, united, free, or kind?

18

Ask God for Good Gifts

Accompanying Scripture Reading: Matthew 7:7–14

A YOUNG BOY NAMED Liam harbored a profound desire, one that went beyond material possessions. He longed for more time with his dad who, due to work commitments, seemed constantly occupied. What Liam didn't understand was that his father was self-employed. He had the power to work the number of hours he wanted to work. Liam's dad, a dedicated provider, often spoke about the importance of hard work. Fearing his dad's disapproval and the strain it might place on their already busy lives, Liam kept his heartfelt wish to himself. As the days and weeks went by, the ache in Liam's heart intensified. Finally, on a quiet evening he mustered the courage to sit with his father. With tears in his eyes, Liam shared his longing for more moments together beyond the constraints of work and responsibilities. To Liam's surprise, his dad's reaction wasn't frustration or

The Life

disappointment but a compassionate understanding. Embracing his son, Liam's dad acknowledged the importance of their bond and expressed excitement about spending more time with his son.

God is not busy. He doesn't run short of time or money. When we avoid asking God for things out of fear of putting him out, we show that our view of God is too small.

I hate asking for things. I'm an Enneagram three, so I would much prefer to impress people with how little I need than appear to be needy. But how ignorant is that? Our filthy-rich, crazy-powerful Heavenly Father tells us to ask him for stuff and we don't do it. Jesus tells us to ask him for what we want:

> Keep on asking, and you will receive what you ask for. Keep on seeking, and you will find. Keep on knocking, and the door will be opened to you. For everyone who asks, receives. Everyone who seeks, finds. And to everyone who knocks, the door will be opened. (Matt 7:7–8)

This passage is difficult for me because I have been burned by the prosperity gospel. Preachers have told me I'm not getting what I ask for from God because there is too much sin in my life or because I don't have enough faith. I have spent too many years trying to contort my brain to believe more, to make my faith more blind and naïve.

One of the teachers at my Christian high school convinced me that, if I believed enough, God would give me a Lamborghini. The problem is that God didn't give me a Lamborghini. In fact, I drive a minivan. Yes, I'm that guy. But what did God give me? He gave me the realization that it would be really dumb for me to have a Lamborghini. My son's car seat wouldn't fit.

As my faith has matured (and that is a work in progress), the things I ask for in prayer have changed. In fact, every day I start my quiet time prayer with this: "God, what do you want me to pray about?" And the prayer that he gives me is almost never about me. As a result, my prayers have become less focused on me and more focused on others. I spend more time in intercession, in prayer for other people.

God answers our prayers. Sometimes his answer is "yes." Sometimes it's "no." Today's passage is about the good gifts that God gives his children, but only he truly knows which gifts are good gifts.

In the chapter before today's passage, Jesus told us how not to pray:

Ask God for Good Gifts

> When you pray, don't babble on and on as the Gentiles do. They think their prayers are answered merely by repeating their words again and again. Don't be like them, for your Father knows exactly what you need even before you ask him! (Matt 6:7-8)

The question then becomes, if God already knows what we need, why does he want us to ask? To answer that, I need to give three of the reasons we should pray:

1. Relationship

Prayer is about much more than getting things from God. The primary purpose of prayer is relationship. There is no greater blessing that we can receive than the blessing of a relationship with the God of the universe. If I pray to God to ask him for a Lamborghini, but neglect a relationship with the one who I am praying to, I have sacrificed something great to potentially get something small.

2. Obedience

A second reason to pray is obedience. The Bible commands us to pray. Even when we don't understand why God commands us to do something, we do it because we have faith that his plans are better than our plans. The great heroes of the Christian faith prayed even after they received clear instructions from God. Moses, David, Jeremiah, and even Jesus prayed.

3. Humility

Prayer humbles us. It reminds us of our limits and God's sovereignty. God knows what we need. However, to invest in our relationship with God, remain obedient to him, and humble ourselves before him, we pray.

> Humble yourselves before the Lord, and he will lift you up in honor. (Jas 4:10)

If God gives us good gifts, and if he lifts us up in honor, we would be wise to bring bold and extravagant requests to God. Christ told us to ask for the things we want, and those requests do impact God's actions:

> You don't have what you want because you don't ask God for it. (Jas 4:2)

Apparently, God has good gifts that he wants to give us, but he will not give them to us unless we ask. I don't entirely understand why, but that is what he does.

Reflect: What holds you back from asking God for more—forgetfulness, doubt, shame, anger, fear of disappointment, or something else?

19

The Church Is a Rock

Accompanying Scripture Reading: Matthew 7:15–29

WHEN YOU HEAR THE word "church," what do you think of? You might think of a white building with a steeple on top, a stage with lights and a fog machine, or a living room with a TV playing church online. Others might think of an NFL stadium, where they go to church on Sundays to worship big, sweaty men. When we read the word "church" in the New Testament, it is translated from the Greek word *ekklesia*. An *ekklesia* is simply a gathering of people united by common identity and purpose. So, fans at an NFL game are definitely an *ekklesia*. The Republican Convention is an *ekklesia*. Swifties at a Taylor Swift concert are an *ekklesia*. This description reveals that an *ekklesia* is not a location. It's people. It's dynamic. It's active.

In AD 313, Constantine made Christianity mainstream and that changed everything. When that happened, the church started to shift from

The Life

a movement, to a location, to an institution. Eventually, to reflect this new church identity, the church took a German word and forced it into Greek verses in the Bible. That German word is *kirche*, and it describes a location. That's where we get the word church.

Ekklesia and *kirche* convey very different ideas. You can lock the doors of a *kirche*, not an *ekklesia*. In fact, if you try to lock the doors on an *ekklesia*, the movement will grow. It will become more attractive. That's what makes Christianity so amazing. No other *ekklesia* has grown so relentlessly.

The Christian church is not an organization that has a limited growth curve. It is alive. It is the bride of Christ and it is built on an unbreakable foundation. Jesus told the apostles that the foundation of the church is a solid rock:

> Upon this rock I will build my church, and all the powers of hell will not conquer it. (Matt 16:18)

The relentless growth of the church is proof that God is in charge of it:

> If their purpose or activity is of human origin, it will fail. But if it is from God, you will not be able to stop these men; you will only find yourselves fighting against God. (Acts 5:38–39)

When Jesus was killed, his followers went back to their old lives. They abandoned the movement. If Christ is dead, there is no Christianity. If Jesus was dead, he was simply a liar who could do magic tricks. The resurrection of Jesus changed everything.

> Anyone who listens to my teaching and follows it is wise, like a person who builds a house on solid rock. (Matt 7:24)

The strength of the church is evidence that Jesus is who he said he is. Christians who follow the teachings of Jesus live better lives. They get fewer divorces.[1] They commit suicide at a much lower rate.[2] They are less depressed,[3] and they break fewer laws[4] (largely because many of our laws come from the Christian Bible).

The story of the prodigal son is an excellent illustration of the effectiveness of biblical teaching (Luke 15:11–32). When the prodigal son ran away from home, he did everything he had fantasized about doing. He lived

1. Stanton, "FactChecker: Divorce Rate."
2. Kumar, "Church Attendance."
3. Belling, "Going to Church Often."
4. "Effects of Religious Practice."

life according to the world's way, not Christ's way. Eventually, he concluded he wanted to go back home to his dad. Why? Because his dad's way of living was better. It worked. It may have seemed boring but it was beautiful. It was effective.

Many people have decided that church isn't worth it. They've considered the amount of time it takes to get involved in church, the guilt they feel when they come to a church gathering, and the number of sporting events they would have to skip. They have chosen comfort over growth.

I shouldn't be embarrassed to tell you I failed seventh grade, but I am. I had to take it twice. It was bad enough the first time around, but the second time was almost unbearable. All my friends moved on to eighth grade, I had to make friends with the bratty sixth graders because now I was one of them! Can you guess what happened the second time I was in seventh grade? I got straight As, and it wasn't just because I had already learned all the seventh grade stuff or because I got smarter. It's because I learned how to study. I had to work harder than other kids to get the same grades, but I never wanted to experience the pain of getting held back again. I decided I was going to study harder than everyone else. I learned my lesson. In fact, I got straight As all the way through school. I was the valedictorian of my class, not because I'm smart, but because I had learned a valuable lesson.

Have you ever experienced failure and thought, "There's got to be a better way." During my second time in seventh grade, I was also the starting point guard on the basketball team. I was shorter than everyone else, but I figured out that I could make myself valuable to the team by being a good passer. The problem was, even though I was a year older than everyone else in the class, they all hit puberty before I did. I was a late bloomer. Evan, the backup point guard, was not a late bloomer. Soon enough, Evan took my place in the starting lineup. Evan could pass too, but he was six inches taller than me.

So, I decided that I had to find a different way to make a name for myself in high school. That's when I traded basketball for music. I tried out for a band, bought a guitar, and I lived in my bedroom learning to play guitar and sing. That got me to the eleventh grade. In other words, it got me to puberty. So, I had a second chance at basketball, and I had a new skill.

We all face turning points in life where we realize there's got to be a better way, and it's our reactions to these moments that make the biggest impact on our future.

Christians, we should regularly reflect on the outcomes of our actions. If we don't, we end up failing over and over. Instead, let's live so well that the demons get mad at our joy, our health, our beauty, our love. God's way works, and sin is always rooted in the idea that we are better than God at making us happy.

At some point, every married guy I know has been tempted to think they would be happier with multiple sex partners. God says we'll be happier with one. He's not a prude. He just knows what works best because he created us.

Follow his teaching and build your life on the solid rock of his wisdom, on the solid foundation of his truth. Storms are coming. Pain is coming, but those things are temporary. If we want God's blessing, we will follow his teachings. Then, when the storms come, we will thrive. We will endure, not only because we obeyed, but also because he will be there with us. Never let the presence of a storm cause you to doubt the presence of God.

The promise of the Christian church is that God can be more effective in our lives when we are active members of his church. God shows up in different ways when we're together:

> For where two or three gather together as my followers, I am there among them. (Matt 18:20)

I've heard people say, "The mountains are my church," but let me respectfully say, "They are not." The church is a gathering of people, not of dirt. The mountains are a great place to worship and connect with God, but there is a unique spiritual experience in the church that's not available when we're alone:

> And let us not neglect our meeting together, as some people do. (Heb 10:25)

We can't find spiritual blind spots without other believers. When someone is preaching and it makes us mad, there's a good chance they have hit our blind spot. That's called conviction, and it's a good thing. We usually run from it, but we should run to it. That's what Jesus taught. The preached word is a mirror:

> An open rebuke is better than hidden love! Wounds from a sincere friend are better than many kisses from an enemy. (Prov 27:5–6)

Christians, we are priests, and priests preach. They minister to the Lord, and they minister to others. How are you going to minister to others if you're alone in the mountains? Humans were designed to become like the people we're with. We're sponges. We adopt the habits and accents of the people that surround us. If you only spend time with unwise people, you'll become like them.

Show me your friends, and I'll show you your future. So don't just come to church; be the church. My prayer is that you will fully give yourself to the Christian mission and become the person God created you to be. Not for your glory, but for his.

Reflect: Is there anything your family has prioritized over investing in God's church? If so, why?

20

Sinners Need Miracles

Accompanying Scripture Reading: Matthew 8:1–17

There is a story in Matt 8 about a time that Jesus healed a Roman centurion's slave boy. I have struggled with this story a lot.

After Jesus returned to Capernaum, a Roman centurion approached him, asking Jesus to heal his servant boy who was in terrible pain. A centurion is a military commander with one hundred soldiers serving under him. In Jesus' time, they were Rome's best warriors, Rome's Goliaths, and they were the enemy occupying Israel. Despite the uncomfortable political situation, Jesus offered to go with him to heal the servant, but the officer pushed back on Jesus' offer:

> But the officer said, "Lord, I am not worthy to have you come into my home. Just say the word from where you are, and my servant will be healed. I know this because I am under the authority of my superior officers, and I have authority over my soldiers. I only

Sinners Need Miracles

need to say, 'Go,' and they go, or 'Come,' and they come. And if I say to my slaves, 'Do this,' they do it." (Matt 8:8–9)

Apparently, there were things in this centurion's home he didn't want Jesus to see, but that didn't deter Jesus. In fact, Jesus praised the officer's faith:

When Jesus heard this, he was amazed. Turning to those who were following him, he said, "I tell you the truth, I haven't seen faith like this in all Israel!" (Matt 8:10)

Then Jesus healed the young servant boy from where he was.

In this story, the centurion used the Greek word *pais* to reference this sick boy. *Pais* translates to "my young servant." Luke, in his version of the story, used the Greek word *doulos*, which means "slave." This is significant because, in their culture, these two Greek words refer to two different kinds of slaves. Slavery in that time didn't have racial overtones like it does today. It had economic overtones. It was all about fortune and indebtedness. The whole first century was built on slavery. It's one of the great evils of history.

One of the things that I wrestle with in this story is the fact that Jesus did so little to fight slavery. Instead, he focused on the gospel. There's a leadership lesson here for us. There are a lot of good things we could do, but we're wise to stay focused on the best things. It's the "ends" versus the "means." Jesus is in the "ends" business, not the "means" business. He had a goal, and if he had spent his time trying to abolish slavery, he would have failed to reach his goal. The slavery battle would come later.

This centurion clearly had an emotional connection to this boy. He had a lot of love and affection for him. But the boy was still his slave. Yet how does Jesus respond to the centurion's request? He healed him. He didn't say, "I'll heal him if you repent," or "if you free your slaves." He didn't say, "I'll come to your house if you give up your immoral lifestyle." In fact, he said this sinful centurion had the most faith of anyone in Israel. The centurion's faith in Jesus was so great that he knew Jesus could do more than what he led the people around him to believe he could do. I want that kind of faith.

Jesus was more concerned with the centurion's faith than he was with the centurion's sin. In Jesus' eyes we are all sinners. None of us deserve anything from God, yet in God's grace, he gives what we don't deserve. We are tempted to create hierarchies of sin because we recognize that some sins have worse consequences in this world, but Jesus recognizes that every sin that is not forgiven will cause the ultimate pain.

Contrary to the teachings of many prosperity gospel preachers, Jesus didn't use prerequisites for healing. He healed out of kindness, out of love.

Jesus chose to heal the boy, even if it meant he had to go back to a life of slavery. When Jesus saves us, he doesn't rescue us from the pain of this world. Because we have lessons to learn, and God has glory to receive, God allows us to persevere through pain. If God sanctified us entirely, if he removed pain from our lives, the world would begin to glorify us. They would want to be like us, rather than like Christ. The pain of this world reminds us that our hope is not in this world. We need to be unhappy with the way things are here so that we desire heaven.

We are all sinners in need of a savior. We are all sick people in need of a doctor. Can we look at sinful people not as less than, but as sinners in need of Jesus just like us? When we see people who commit sins that we think are worse than ours, how do we react? Do we love them in their sin? Jesus did.

We also see in this story the value of persistent prayer. We read about multiple interactions in the life of Christ that demonstrate God's willingness to change his plan to grant the requests of people. Because I have received so many "nos" from God, I sometimes shy away from bringing more requests to him, and I fail to ask persistently. Other times, I think I can't ask God for things because there is a sin issue in my life. In the past, I have felt too guilty to bring my requests to God, but that isn't how God works. He will give good gifts to his children even when they are rebellious. He gives good gifts because he is righteous, not because we are righteous. That is why we put our faith in him, not in ourselves.

My prayer today is that our faith in God will grow bigger than our sinful temptations and habits.

Reflect: Do you find yourself tempted to treat a particular sin as worse than others, thereby excluding people who commit that sin from full fellowship with God?

21

God Has a Green Thumb

Accompanying Scripture Reading: Matthew 13:1–23

MY MOM HAS A green thumb. My wife and I, on the other hand, kill plants often. Once, after we killed a plant, we decided to throw it away. However, when my mom found it in the dumpster, she said, "Wait, let me try to save it." Today, that plant is huge. She took a small piece of the plant that was still alive, replanted it, and nourished it to health.

I believe something that is somewhat controversial. I believe God has a green thumb. If God's seed is planted in you, it will grow. If you let it, it will change you. He will make it grow. The process is outlined by the apostle Paul:

> I planted the seed, Apollos watered it, but God has been making it grow. So neither the one who plants nor the one who waters is anything, but only God, who makes things grow. (1 Cor 3:6–7)

I am a Wesleyan, and Wesleyans are often tempted to make everything about our free will, but we also believe God is sovereign. He does give us free will, but when we are his children, he changes us.

When we are in a relationship with Jesus, it changes everything. Our entire identity changes. It's not about our knowledge; it's about our relationship with him. All the major monotheistic religions of the world claim to believe in the God of Abraham: the Jews, the Muslims (both Shia and Sunni), and the Christians, but only Christians have a personal relationship with him.

If I jumped the fence at the White House, would the guards stop me and keep me from going in? Of course they would. What if (like Buddy the Elf talking about Santa) I said, "It's ok, I know the president"? The secret service would say, "I don't care who you know. You can't come in." However, if the president looked out the White House window and said, "It's okay. I know Mike Wilson. Let him in," the guards would absolutely let me in. What really matters is not that I know him, it's that he knows me. Why? Because he's the one with the power:

> You say you have faith, for you believe that there is one God. Good for you! Even the demons believe this, and they tremble in terror. (Jas 2:19)

Our salvation is not acquired by knowing who God is. Our salvation is accomplished by being known by God, by having a relationship with him. Do you have a relationship with Jesus? Jesus talked to his followers about the effect of being in a relationship with him:

> A good tree produces good fruit, and a bad tree produces bad fruit. A good tree can't produce bad fruit, and a bad tree can't produce good fruit. So every tree that does not produce good fruit is chopped down and thrown into the fire. (Matt 7:17–19)

As I write this, I am sitting in my living room. There are two plants in the room. One is healthy, but imperfect. It has some dead leaves and it leans to the left. The other plant is perfect. Every leaf is perfectly green and it stands straight. There's just one problem. The perfect plant is fake. It looks perfect, but it's dead.

Some people are Christian in name only. Like fake plants, they look like they are alive, but they are spiritually dead. Like a politician who claims to be a Christian to get votes, they have alternative motives in claiming to know Jesus. We can look at these fake Christians and recognize they are fake by the lack of fruit they produce. To identify Christians, we look for the fruits of love, joy, peace, patience, kindness, goodness, faithfulness, gentleness, and self-control.

We can produce other fruits, but if we appear before Jesus on judgment day bragging about those fruits, we will reveal that we had no relationship with him:

> Not everyone who calls out to me, "Lord! Lord!" will enter the Kingdom of Heaven. Only those who actually do the will of my Father in heaven will enter. On judgment day many will say to me, "Lord! Lord! We prophesied in your name and cast out demons in your name and performed many miracles in your name." But I will reply, "I never knew you. Get away from me, you who break God's laws." (Matt 7:21–22)

One of Jesus' most famous parables is about seeds becoming fruit-producing plants. Matthew 13:3–9 is a parable often referred to as the Parable of the Sower. In it, Jesus tells a story about a sower who goes out to sow seeds. Some seeds fall along the path and are eaten by birds, some fall on rocky ground and wither, some fall among thorns and are choked, but some fall on good soil and produce a fruitful crop. The unique thing about this parable is that Jesus interprets it for us:

> The seed that fell on the footpath represents those who hear the message about the Kingdom and don't understand it. Then the evil one comes and snatches away the seed that was planted in their hearts. The seed on the rocky soil represents those who hear the message and immediately receive it with joy. But since they don't have deep roots, they don't last long. They fall away as soon as they have problems or are persecuted for believing God's word. The seed that fell among the thorns represents those who hear God's word, but all too quickly the message is crowded out by the worries of this life and the lure of wealth, so no fruit is produced. The seed that fell on good soil represents those who truly hear and understand God's word and produce a harvest of thirty, sixty, or even a hundred times as much as had been planted! (Matt 13:19–23)

Jesus is the sower. He reveals the truth, but the truth seems like foolishness to some. Jesus tells the truth and the satan tells lies. If we reject Jesus' truth, or if we don't listen to it long enough to understand it, the satan will take us right to hell with him.

Some people sign up to join the Christians, but they don't know what they are agreeing to. Maybe they follow Jesus because of an emotional event or to follow a friend. Others choose to join the Christians because they like the music or because it makes them feel good. That's consumer Christianity and it doesn't last. If they don't mature past consumer Christianity, they turn their back on Jesus as soon as they don't get what they want.

Jesus listed two types of thorns that distract people from developing a relationship with him: the worries of life and the lure of wealth. If our attention is on the worries of this life, it is because we've taken our eyes off Christ and his goodness. The birds and lilies trust God, so should we. Similarly, if our focus is on power and wealth, they will eventually take our loyalty from God. It is very difficult for a rich person to enter the kingdom of God. Do you have ears to hear God's word? If you do, you will produce fruit.

Let me also add some encouragement. Please do not allow this parable to cause you to doubt your salvation. If you feel convicted, that is the method Jesus is using to produce fruit in your life. Run to Jesus, not away from him. Let conviction lead you to a deeper relationship with Jesus.

Reflect: Which fruit of the Spirit (love, joy, peace, patience, kindness, goodness, faithfulness, gentleness, self-control) is most evident in your life, and which is least evident?

22

How to Be Healed

Accompanying Scripture Reading: John 5:1–9

IN JOHN 5:1–15, THERE is a story about Jesus healing a crippled man by the pool of Bethesda. The passage describes the location of the pool in detail. It states that the pool was inside the city near the sheep gate and had five covered porches. That description is important because for centuries there was no evidence the pool ever existed. Skeptics used its nonexistence as proof that the book of John was written by some zealot, not by the apostle John. That is until archeologists found the Pool of Bethesda in 1888.[1] It is right by the Sheep Gate and, because it has two separate bathing areas, it has five porches. Trust your Bible.

The pool was built in the eighth century BC by damming up rainwater in a valley. That means the pool qualified as a mikvah. In Jewish tradition,

1. "Pool of Bethesda."

a mikvah is a pool of natural water in which one bathes for the restoration of ritual purity. The water was called natural because the water flowed naturally into the pool. It was not gathered by hand. This water was also referred to as living water or holy water. If living water is water gathered without human effort, what does that say about God offering us living water? A few verses before this story, Jesus offered living water to the woman at the well:

> But those who drink the water I give will never be thirsty again. It becomes a fresh, bubbling spring within them, giving them eternal life. (John 4:14)

In this verse, Jesus gave us a metaphor of his gift of grace. We can't earn it. It is a gift. Like the water in the mikvah, Jesus produces it and gives it to us.

This mikvah, though, was unique. The locals believed that it had the ability to heal people:

> 3Crowds of sick people—blind, lame, or paralyzed—lay on the porches. 5One of the men lying there had been sick for thirty-eight years. (John 5:3, 5)

Did you catch it? We read verse 3 and 5, but there was no verse 4. The translation above is the New Living Translation. This translation, along with many other translations, has removed verse 4 because it is not in the oldest manuscripts of the Bible. However, the New International Version does include verse 4. Let's read verse 4 in the New International Version:

> (Some manuscripts include here, wholly or in part) paralyzed—and they waited for the moving of the waters. 4From time to time an angel of the Lord would come down and stir up the waters. The first one into the pool after each such disturbance would be cured of whatever disease they had. (John 5:4 NIV)

If this verse was not written by John, who added it, and what was the motivation? Who actually stirred the waters and healed people? The translators of the New International Version say it was an angel, but many people in Jesus' day believed that it was another god.

Many people in Jesus' day were members of the cult of Asclepius.[2] They built temples for the serpent spirits by mikvahs, and they believed serpents would churn the waters and heal people.[3] The Greeks attributed

2. Lizorkin-Eyzenberg, "Healing Center of Asclepius."
3. Bryan, "Pool Strangely Stirred."

How to Be Healed

the healing power to natural occurrences, to chemicals in natural springs.[4] Others theorize that it was all superstition and no one was actually healed.

Jesus, however, said he was the source of living water. When he saw the sick man who had been ill for thirty-eight years, he asked him if he would like to get well. The answer to that question seems obvious, but I think Jesus knew more about this man's situation than we do. Jesus was asking him if he was comfortable. He wanted to know if this man wanted to keep putting his faith in the pool, or if he was ready to put his faith in God. Jesus was challenging Asclepius.

The sick man told Jesus that he was incapable of getting into the pool when the water bubbled up. Apparently, he was still looking to the pool for healing. He didn't realize the source of the power he was so desperate for was standing right in front of him.

Then the sick man brought up another excuse. He said someone else always got in the pool before him. Everyone was looking out for themselves. Apparently, adherents to the cult of Asclepius weren't in the habit of putting others before themselves. Jesus was undeterred by the sick man's excuses:

Jesus told him, "Stand up, pick up your mat, and walk!" (John 5:8)

Notice that this man did not pray a prayer of salvation before Jesus healed him. He didn't confess his sins. He didn't even put his faith in Jesus, but Jesus healed him. Then the man rolled up his bed and began to walk.

We have been invited to look to Jesus. The world offers us solutions to our problems that will only lead us to more pain. They ask us to look inside ourselves for meaning and hope, but we are crippled, incapable of healing ourselves. We are lost, and the only way to be found is to surrender to Christ.

A couple of years ago, my wife, Darci, my two sons, Lincoln and Titus, and I went to Disney World. Darci and I were talking as we stood in line for the Peter Pan ride when I looked down and realized Lincoln was no longer standing by us.

If you have ever lost a child, you know that it takes no time for your heart to start beating faster. We were in a huge crowd and I was separated from our son. I imagine God feels this way when his children turn their back on him. Separation from your children brings excruciating pain.

Darci and I started yelling and frantically looking all around us, but we could not find him. Then, a little boy standing behind us pointed down

---

4. Griffin, "Did Jesus or the Pool?"

the path and said, "He ran." So I ran. I ran faster than I could run. I was literally shoving people out of my way. After what seemed like ten minutes (but was really ten seconds), I saw Lincoln far down the path with a guy who was wearing clothes that looked like mine. I was still pretty far from him, but I could see that Lincoln was crying very hard. When he realized the man he was chasing wasn't me, he was overwhelmed with fear. When I finally reached him, he grabbed me and said, "You left me." I replied, "No ... your mom left you." No, I didn't say that. I said, "Son, I will never leave you." Lincoln thought that he was chasing me, but by chasing someone he thought was me, he ran away from me.

Compare this story to your relationship with God. We spend so much of our lives searching for solutions to our problems, healing for our pain, and answers to our questions. God has all of these for us. The world offers solutions to our problems, but it can only give us more pain.

This sick man by the pool looked to the pool for healing, but the only one who could ever heal him was standing right beside him. The man chased after the wrong healer.

When it comes to following, there are a lot of options. Every politician, every pyramid scheme, and every celebrity wants you to follow them, but none of them can heal you. None of them can save you. Follow Jesus.

Reflect: What is competing with God for your loyalty—politics, entertainment, sports, relationships, money, celebrity culture, or something else?

23

Be Made Whole

Accompanying Scripture Reading: John 5:5–30

When John described the sick man at the Pool of Bethesda in John 5, he told us that the man was sick for thirty-eight years, not that he sat by the pool for thirty-eight years. Based on what we know about life expectancy at this time, it is likely that this man was sick his entire life, or at least most of his life. He was an old man in their community. A life of illness was the only life he knew.

My home television is often turned to the golf channel, which means that we watch the senior tour when there aren't other tournaments happening. Golf is unique because it is one of the few sports in which senior competition gets public attention. Can you imagine if seniors continued to play other sports . . . like mixed martial arts? A twenty-year-old can fight in

The Life

the cage for hours, but an old man fight would be a death match. I wouldn't be able to sleep if I knew there was a senior citizen UFC fight on TV.

That's what I picture when I think about the sick man fighting to get into the pool when the waters of the Pool of Bethesda began to churn, but everything changed when the old man encountered Jesus:

> When Jesus saw him and knew he had been ill for a long time, he asked him, "Would you like to get well?" (John 5:6)

Sometimes, we complain about things in our lives that we are not willing to change. When we see ourselves as overweight, poor, depressed, lonely, childless, or overwhelmed, Jesus asks us, "Would you like to get well?" When we have our own idea of how life should be lived, Jesus confronts us with an alternative solution.

When Jesus healed the man at the Pool of Bethesda, you would assume everyone who witnessed the event would celebrate and choose to follow Jesus. However, that is not how the religious leaders responded. Because Jesus performed the miracle on the Sabbath, the Jewish leaders objected. When the Jewish leaders saw the man who had been cured carrying his bed, they reprimanded him for carrying his bed on the Sabbath.

After the prophets wrote the Hebrew Scriptures, rabbis added oral traditions, laws, and interpretations to the collection of holy writings. These rabbinic writings added to the laws that we see today in the Old Testament, and they took the Sabbath laws to the extreme. For example, one of these laws literally forbade people from carrying their bed on a Sabbath. The Sabbath was no longer about honoring God. Instead, it was about appearing to be righteous.

Jesus knew the oral traditions. He knew that carrying your bed on the Sabbath was forbidden. So why did Jesus heal this man on the Sabbath? He could have come back the next day or simply told the man to wait until the next day to carry his bed. Instead, Jesus instructed the man to break this Sabbath law. Jesus was teaching us that sometimes it is necessary to break a law, especially a religious law.

Growing up, my church used the word "sanctuary" to describe the large room where we gathered to worship on Sundays, and there were special rules for the sanctuary. For example, we were instructed to never stand on the altar, drink in the sanctuary, wear a hat in "God's house," or eat all the extra communion bread. Okay, that last one might have been necessary.

What is a sanctuary? A sanctuary is a holy place or a place that provides protection, and that is why it is a terrible name for the Christian church to use to describe a room. The church building is not God's house. We are God's house, his holy temple. God has tabernacles in us:

> Don't you realize that all of you together are the temple of God and that the Spirit of God lives in you? God will destroy anyone who destroys this temple. For God's temple is holy, and you are that temple. (1 Cor 3:16–17)

In addition, the church building should not be a place for Christians to bunker for safety. We are not commanded to separate from the world, but to be in the world. We cannot complete our Great Commission without interacting with the world. When we cower in fear, we are ineffective.

Sanctuary language implies that God's home is in the church building and that he stays there, and if God stays in the church building, so does our faith. That is why our church chooses to use the word "auditorium" to refer to the big room in which we gather on Sundays to worship. God, and the ability to worship him, is not confined to a building.

We choose not to act differently in the auditorium than everywhere else because God is with us wherever we are. God is everywhere. For that reason, we choose to break sanctuary rules. I believe Jesus had similar motivations when he instructed the man to carry his bed on the Sabbath:

> But he replied, "The man who healed me told me, 'Pick up your mat and walk.'" "Who said such a thing as that?" they demanded. The man didn't know, for Jesus had disappeared into the crowd. (John 5:11–13)

So far, this interaction with the sick man has almost nothing to do with the gospel message that is preached in churches today. The man was healed without confessing sins, without praying a prayer of salvation, or even without putting faith in Jesus. Usually when Jesus healed people, he told them that he healed them because of their faith.

It also appears that Jesus is disregarding the law and encouraging this man to misbehave, but that is not the end of the story:

> But afterward Jesus found him in the Temple and told him, "Now you are well; so stop sinning, or something even worse may happen to you." (John 5:14)

THE LIFE

Jesus did not heal this man to lead him to rebellion. He healed him to lead the man to repentance. Jesus was inviting the man to a journey of sanctification. It wasn't enough to recognize that Jesus was the source of life. Jesus invited him to surrender to the source of life. You can't fully experience the life that Christ offers us without following his plan for life, and sin is rebelling against God's plan for life.

The problem is that religious people often take God's plan and attempt to leverage it for their own gain. That's why the Jewish religious leaders created the oral traditions. They twisted the rules God created to acquire power. That is why Jesus said the Sabbath was never created to hold us back. It was created to improve our lives, to make us more like Christ:

> Then Jesus said to them, "The Sabbath was made to meet the needs of people, and not people to meet the requirements of the Sabbath. So the Son of Man is Lord, even over the Sabbath!" (Mark 2:27–28)

The Lord of life is inviting you to a better life. He is asking you to turn your back on the false gods of this world and live the good life that he designed for you. Jesus didn't just want the sick man to be able to walk. Jesus wanted to make him whole.

A terrible idea that is destroying lives in our world is that people don't change, but that idea is not biblical. It's not even logical, and it's incredibly depressing. You're not stuck the way you are. God created you on purpose, for a purpose.

In John 5:6, Jesus asked the man if he wanted to be made well. The actual Greek word that Jesus used for "well" was *hygies*. This word literally translates to "healthy or whole." Jesus was asking this man if he wanted to be whole. God's promise of salvation isn't that he'll forgive your sins, then leave you screwed up and broken. Jesus wants to make you whole.

Reflect: What are some of the social norms or unwritten rules in our world that are worth rejecting?

24

Unlocking Blessings

Accompanying Scripture Reading: John 6:1–15

JOHN 6 RECOUNTS THE miracle of Jesus feeding a huge crowd of people in Tabgha with five loaves and two fish. When Jesus heard King Herod had killed John the Baptist, he sought solitude and boarded a boat for an isolated place. However, word quickly spread, and many people from nearby villages came to see Jesus. When Jesus saw them, he was deeply moved with compassion and began to teach them. As dusk approached, the disciples told Jesus they were concerned about the remote location and the hour. They asked him to send the people away because they didn't have food for them. Instead, Jesus told the disciples to feed the people, but the only person with any food was a little boy who had five loaves of bread and two fish. Jesus told the boy to bring the food to him and instructed the people to sit down. Then, Jesus looked to heaven and prayed a blessing over the five loaves and two fish. He broke the bread, then gave it to the disciples to distribute among the crowd. To their astonishment, everyone ate their fill, and there were twelve baskets of leftovers collected afterward. This miraculous event fed five thousand men and their families.

When we are generous, we get to physically participate in bringing the kingdom of heaven to earth. Supernatural things happen when we give to God. This boy gave to Jesus, and Jesus blessed his generosity. Jesus commands us to be generous people, and this boy showed us what happens when we are.

1. When we are generous, we honor God.

Everything belongs to God. He doesn't need our money. However, when we give to him, it is an act of worship that brings glory to him. When this boy gave his lunch to Jesus, he honored him. Jesus didn't need the bread and fish, but he was honored by them.

> But remember the Lord your God, for it is he who gives you the ability to produce wealth, and so confirms his covenant, which he swore to your ancestors, as it is today. (Deut 8:18 NIV)

Throughout the Bible, when it comes to our possessions, we are first commanded to give back to God. In fact, the word "firstfruits" is used over thirty times in the Bible. Do you know how many times the word "lastfruits" is used? Zero. It's not a word. God asks us to give our firstfruits because our hearts are connected to our treasure. Jesus said that we should store our treasure in heaven rather than on earth:

> Don't store up treasures here on earth, where moths eat them and rust destroys them, and where thieves break in and steal. Store your treasures in heaven, where moths and rust cannot destroy, and thieves do not break in and steal. Wherever your treasure is, there the desires of your heart will also be. (Matt 6:19–21)

This is why we spend so much money on our kids. We love them, so our hearts are with them. Our hearts and our possessions are intimately connected.

If you have ever started a business, you know that you never stop thinking about it. You're invested in it. Have you ever bought stock in a company? Your heart becomes connected to that company. A few years ago I bought some Microsoft stock. I figured they have got to start cutting into

Apple's business eventually. So, even though I've always been an Apple guy, I cheer for Microsoft to produce a phone that can compete with the iPhone.

When you give to God's work, it connects your heart to his work. There is nothing better for your heart than to be connected to God! When the boy gave his lunch to Jesus, it connected him to Jesus' miracle.

The biblical instruction for giving back to God is tithing. Tithing is giving ten percent of your income as an offering to God. If you've never experienced the blessings of tithing, it can sound daunting. There are so many things in this world begging for our money, and tithing requires us to decide to sacrifice the comfort of having things that others have.

In today's story, Jesus made a generosity plan. He didn't just hope something would happen. He gave the disciples instructions, and when they obeyed, he invited the boy to join the plan. When the boy was generous, the disciples laid out the plan for the people, and the stage was set for Jesus to work a miracle.

Do you have a generosity plan?

Parents, isn't your heart full when you see your kids do something generous? My two sons regularly fight over toys. A toy can sit in the toy box for a year; neither kid wants to play with it until one of them wants to play with it. As soon as Lincoln starts playing with a toy, Titus wants it. Then we have to set a timer to take turns with a toy they haven't played with for a year. Yet, occasionally, something amazing happens. On rare occasions, when one of them is playing with a toy, the other one asks for the toy and the one who had the toy first says, "Yes!" I almost pass out every time it happens, but I am filled with pride when I see it.

The ironic thing is that I own the toy they are sharing with each other. I bought it. Can you imagine how God feels when he sees his children giving away what he gave us? God owns everything, and when we give like God gave, we honor him.

This boy in the Tabgha story modeled this for us. Because he was generous, thousands of people were fed. In addition, they got to see a miracle.

2. When we give, we bless others.

My sons enjoy watching Mr. Beast videos on YouTube, primarily because they can't imagine someone giving away their money the way he does. Mr. Beast is making money by being generous, and he is being generous because he is making money.

Blake Mycoskie, the founder of Toms Shoes, similarly discovered that generosity can be a lucrative business. Toms Shoes gives shoes to people who can't afford them, and humans are naturally drawn to generous people.

Ninety-five percent of practicing Christians donate to charity, but only 51 percent of non-Christians donate to charity.[1] Christians are much more generous than the average person, and that's even true about generosity to non-religious charities. If our government tried to replace the services the church provides, it would go bankrupt. The church works because Christians give. This has been the case ever since the Christian church was launched. The early church pooled their money to help people in need:

> There were no needy people among them, because those who owned land or houses would sell them and bring the money to the apostles to give to those in need. (Acts 4:34–35)

Take a few seconds to think of a special gift you have received. How did that gift make you feel?

I remember when I got a Schwinn bike for my eighth birthday. My parents were very poor when I was young. Every month we spent our money before we earned it. The whole family knew when payday was, so I knew how much my parents sacrificed to get me that bike. To this day, it makes me emotional.

When you give to the Christian church, you bless people, and you bless God.

But it doesn't stop there.

3. When we give, we are blessed.

When Jesus used the boy's food to bless many people, the boy was also blessed. His generosity was the talk of the town.

The promise of Mal 3:10 applies to us today:

> "Bring all the tithes into the storehouse so there will be enough food in my Temple. If you do," says the Lord of Heaven's Armies, "I will open the windows of heaven for you. I will pour out a blessing so great you won't have enough room to take it in! Try it! Put me to the test!" (Mal 3:10)

If you don't believe him, he invites you to test him. Try it. Give the first ten percent of your income to God and see what happens. The passage says

---

1. Foley, "Practicing Christians Give More."

that all the nations will call you blessed! You won't just be blessed if you put God first, you will be obviously blessed. Let God bless you.

Reflect: What is your generosity plan?

25

In His Hands

Accompanying Scripture Reading: Luke 8:22–55

THE PROPHET ISAIAH GIVES us many messianic prophecies that clearly point to Jesus and his kingdom. Jesus is in charge. Justice flows freely from his throne. He sits in heaven and mourns for his enemies. He is not afraid of them. They have no power. They cannot be compared to him, and he cares for them!

> For a child is born to us, a son is given to us. The government will rest on his shoulders. And he will be called: Wonderful Counselor, Mighty God, Everlasting Father, Prince of Peace. (Isa 9:6)

This prophecy caused the Jews to believe the Messiah would be a military or political leader. That's why they missed Jesus. When Jesus didn't fight against Rome, the Jews rejected him. It didn't matter how many miracles he performed; they couldn't get past their preconceived notions.

However, Christ's government, his kingdom, was greater than they could have imagined.

Even John the Baptist thought Jesus would use physical power or politics to keep John, the prophesied prophet, out of jail:

> John the Baptist, who was in prison, heard about all the things the Messiah was doing. So he sent his disciples to ask Jesus, "Are you the Messiah we've been expecting, or should we keep looking for someone else? (Matt 11:2–3)

Jesus had demonstrated his sovereignty through his teachings and his miracles, but because Jesus chose not to fight political battles, John began to doubt him. We must remember to trust his plan. His kingdom reigns supreme and his power is unmatched. He holds everything in his hands.

I'm tempted to sing a song I learned in Sunday School. "He's got the whole world in his hands. He's got Jessica, Seth, and Caleb (we all hoped the teacher would say our name next) in his hands. He's got the whole world in his hands."

Luke 8 tells the story of Jesus calming a storm. When the storm hit, the disciples doubted Jesus like John the Baptist did. Storms have a way of causing doubt. Pain causes us to question things we would not have otherwise questioned.

> The disciples went and woke him up, shouting, "Master, Master, we're going to drown!" When Jesus woke up, he rebuked the wind and the raging waves. Suddenly the storm stopped and all was calm. Then he asked them, "Where is your faith?" The disciples were terrified and amazed. "Who is this man?" they asked each other. "When he gives a command, even the wind and waves obey him!" (Luke 8:24–25)

Jesus is in charge. Everyone and everything must obey him, including evil spirits.

Luke 8:26–39 tells a story about a naked, homeless, and demon-possessed man who lived in a tomb. When Jesus talked to the man, the man fell to the ground, and the demon identified himself by the name "legion." In other words, there were thousands of demons in this man. The demons made the man incredibly strong, but even they were no match for Jesus. He cast them into a herd of pigs that ran off a cliff and drowned in a lake.

How would you feel if you were a farmer and someone killed all your pigs? I bet you'd be angry, as were the owners of these pigs. They ran to town to tell everyone, and the people were terrified. When they saw that the man had been healed, they begged Jesus to leave. Jesus' sheer power terrified people. So, Jesus left.

This is how many people react to God today. God invites us to join his kingdom and participate in his power, but some people choose to rule their own weak, temporary kingdom. Rather than allowing God to rule over them, to call the shots in their life, they tell Jesus to get away, and he does.

When Jesus left these people, he went to the other side of the lake where a crowd of people gathered to see him. They had heard about his power and welcomed him with open arms. While he was there, a religious leader named Jairus fell at Jesus' feet and asked Jesus to heal his twelve-year-old daughter. So, Jesus started walking to Jairus' house to heal the girl. While they were walking with a huge crowd around them, a woman snuck up behind Jesus to touch him. She also wanted to be healed because she had a disease that caused her to constantly bleed for twelve years.

The blood flow issue is a picture of sin. I grew up hearing sermons about this story, and preachers always made her sound dignified. They would say, "This woman reached out for God, and we need a generation that will reach out for God. If you seek hard enough, you'll reach God." But I don't think that's the proper reading of this passage. God is showing us how close he is. He comes to us. This passage clarifies that the woman was the one who was sneaking. Those preachers never talked about how God uses sneaky people. Are you embarrassed? Are you sneaking your way to Jesus? Come as you are.

> Coming up behind Jesus, she touched the fringe of his robe. Immediately, the bleeding stopped. "Who touched me?" Jesus asked. Everyone denied it, and Peter said, "Master, this whole crowd is pressing up against you." (Luke 8:44–45)

Jesus didn't ask who touched him because he didn't know. He asked because he wanted her to come out of hiding. He wanted to know her. The lady wasn't on Jesus' schedule. He was going to heal the twelve-year-old girl, but he was happy to change his plans for her. Unfortunately, the glee of this moment was interrupted. While they were celebrating, a messenger came and told Jairus that his daughter had died before they could get to her. If only Jesus hadn't stopped to heal the bleeding woman, then maybe he could have healed the little girl!

> But when Jesus heard what had happened, he said to Jairus, "Don't be afraid. Just have faith, and she will be healed." When they arrived at the house, Jesus wouldn't let anyone go in with him except Peter, John, James, and the little girl's father and mother. The house was filled with people weeping and wailing, but he said, "Stop the weeping! She isn't dead; she's only asleep." (Luke 8:50–52)

The people began to mock Jesus for claiming the girl was only asleep, but Jesus was about to demonstrate his power in a way that these people had never seen:

> Then Jesus took her by the hand and said in a loud voice, "My child, get up!" And at that moment her life returned, and she immediately stood up! (Luke 8:54–55)

Nothing can stand against the power of our God, not storms, demons, illness, or even death. If the storms of life have caused you to doubt God's plan, remind yourself of his sovereignty.

Reflect: What fear or pain do you need to surrender to God today?

26

Staying Faithful in Storms

Accompanying Scripture Reading: Mark 4:26–41

SHIPS DON'T SINK BECAUSE there is water around them; they sink when water gets inside them. Don't let what is happening around you get inside of you and weigh you down.

Many people in Jesus' day were terrified of the sea. They believed giant monsters lived in the sea[1] and that there were portals to hell at the bottom of them.[2] Perhaps Jesus picked fishermen to be his disciples because they were brave. They were brave enough to sit in a tippable boat every day on top of these portals to hell. Or maybe Jesus chose fishermen because they were not superstitious. Non-superstitious people are naturally skeptical. This means they were likely to stay faithful to Jesus when they eventually

1. Steinmeyer, "Biblical Monsters."
2. Richter, "11 Hidden Spots."

believed he was who he said he was. They wouldn't just follow every new, popular superstition.

Mark 4:35-41 tells the story of a day when Jesus and his disciples were in a boat when a storm hit. The disciples were terrified that the boat would sink, but Jesus was asleep at the back of the boat, resting with his head on a pillow. The disciples woke Jesus and asked him why he didn't care if they drowned, but Jesus still wasn't afraid. Instead, he reprimanded the wind and commanded the waves to stop. He told the storm to be quiet, and a profound calm enveloped the sea, and the disciples were amazed. Turning to his disciples, Jesus asked them why they were so scared and why they had so little faith.

> The disciples were absolutely terrified. "Who is this man?" they asked each other. "Even the wind and waves obey him!" (Mark 4:41)

When we talk about Jesus calming the storm, we usually jump to metaphors. The storm is a metaphor of temptation, of pain, or of people who have hurt us. There's value in those, but the real lesson of the story is all about faith. Put your faith in Jesus, and the storms cannot defeat you. Christ's good news is very good. Jesus didn't just help them endure the storm. He calmed the storm.

Now that we're on the other side of the resurrection, we see that Jesus' invitation to put our faith in him isn't about faith for our physical protection, but about faith for eternal protection. We are more than our bodies because faith gives us eternal life. Put your faith in Jesus, and you will live forever. Christians, nothing can kill you. It's not a promise of physical comfort. It's a gift of eternal life.

There are only a few reasons people choose not to put their faith in Jesus. They might be said in many ways, but none of the objections are new objections. Let's wrestle with some of those reasons:

1. Some people doubt God because bad things happen.

People who are skeptical of the Christian God often believe that if God were real, bad things wouldn't happen so often. In other words, they're looking for more miracles. For God to keep bad things from happening, he would have to perform miracles everywhere and always.

I once heard a story about a pastor and a skeptical barber who lived in a small town. They often engaged in spirited discussions about faith and the existence of God. One day, the barber declared, "There's no God; too many bad things happen." Undaunted, the pastor replied, "What makes you think there's no God?" Their conversation continued until the pastor's haircut was finished. As he left the barber shop, the pastor noticed a man with long, untamed hair and a shaggy beard. The pastor invited the man back into the barber shop and said to the barber, "I don't believe barbers exist." Perplexed, the barber asked, "Why not?" The pastor responded, "If barbers exist, why would someone have long hair like this?"

If you don't search for God, you probably won't find him. When God offers a solution to your problems that you don't like, it doesn't mean he didn't offer the solution. It just means you didn't receive the solution. If God tells you that healing your body is not what is best for you, you can choose to believe him or not, but your belief does not change whether he is right or not. In that case, it's not that you don't believe in God, but that you believe you are a god. If we believe God exists, then it's logical to believe that he has a better idea of what is good than we do. If God is real, we shouldn't expect him to follow us. We follow him.

Other people have the opposite problem.

2. Some people doubt God because they are skeptical of miracles.

Rather than expecting God to perform miracles everywhere and all the time, some people don't believe miracles are possible at all.

Sometimes it's hard to believe in God because he does such amazing things, but isn't that what you'd expect from God? If he claimed to create the world, then didn't do any miracles, you would question him. Would you want to worship a limited god; a god who struggles like we do?

The world is hungry, but the world's menu offers no sustenance for the soul. Questions like "How did the world begin?" and "What makes life meaningful?" are met with silence. Even inquiries about the source of our moral compass receive no satisfying answers. Instead, the world presents its enticing menu of airbrushed people, shallow entertainment, and the allure of unbridled indulgence. They entice with flavors that tantalize the taste buds but leave an insatiable hunger within.

In contrast, Christians recognize the profound richness and sustenance of their solution. God came to earth and sacrificed for me, and the world offers me images of superficial beauty and Prozac? It's a profound contrast that highlights the depth of faith in a world that is often consumed by physical pleasures.

3. Some people choose not to put their faith in Jesus because Christians have hurt them.

Choosing not to trust Jesus because other people who trust Jesus make mistakes is an illogical response. The truth is that Christians are statistically better at life than the rest of the world. We're happier, healthier, and much more generous, but that does not always mean all Christians act like Christ. A parent could have three great kids; a bad experience with one of them doesn't mean the parent is bad. It means kids are kids. They're going to make mistakes.

Christians, if we want people to follow God, we need to set a good example of what that looks like. Non-Christians, be patient with us. We will make mistakes, but don't reject God just because we screw up. The problem isn't his leadership. The problem is that sometimes we don't follow well.

Have you ever seen a palm tree in a windstorm? It's amazing to watch as they bend dramatically in the wind. They flex so far that it looks like they will break, but they don't. Palm trees have bounce-back. They can withstand incredible winds because when the wind bends them, they bounce back.[3] Do you have bounce-back? Psalms tells us that is what faith gives us.

> But the godly will flourish like palm trees and grow strong like the cedars of Lebanon. For they are transplanted to the Lord's own house. They flourish in the courts of our God. (Ps 92:12–13)

God allows the storms in our lives because they have a way of growing our faith. Those who are truly God's children grow in storms.

At the triumphal entry, when Jesus rode into Jerusalem on a donkey, people waved palm branches. What they didn't know was that a storm was coming. Some people broke in that storm, but other people saw Jesus' incredible act of love and were strengthened.

We celebrate because Jesus has accomplished everything necessary for us to be his children, to be transplanted to God's own house. Put your faith in him, and the promise of eternal life is yours!

Reflect: What tends to cause you to doubt God's existence or his goodness?

---

3. Geggel, "How Do Palm Trees."

27

Embracing Sea Monsters

Accompanying Scripture Reading: Matthew 14:22–36

I AM AN AMERICAN, and the agenda to redeem America has been a priority of the American church for most of my life. This pursuit has taught me that we're not going to change our country with one major political battle. To change a nation, you have to start by changing the hearts of people.

One man can change the heart of a family. One family can change the heart of a church. One church can change the heart of a city. One city can change the heart of a state. One state can change the heart of a nation. One nation can change the heart of the world, but it all starts with one changed heart. If we want to help our nation, we have to start with our own hearts.

If Christ is not at the center of our life, it doesn't matter who we vote for. What good is freedom if we are going to misuse it to destroy ourselves? True freedom is not about getting to make our own decisions and having control over our own lives. It's about knowing the truth, all blinders removed. Christians, we have to start by getting Jesus into the hearts of people. That's the only way we are going to see positive change in our world.

The story of Jesus walking on water has received a lot of attention throughout history. During my lifetime, John Ortberg preached the most famous sermon on this story. The famous title of that sermon is "If You Want to Walk on Water, You Have to Get Out of the Boat,"[1] but I think that sermon misses the most important lesson of the story.

> [Jesus] saw the disciples straining at the oars, because the wind was against them. Shortly before dawn he went out to them, walking on the lake. He was about to pass by them, but when they saw him walking on the lake, they thought he was a ghost. They cried out, because they all saw him and were terrified. Immediately he spoke to them and said, "Take courage! It is I. Don't be afraid." Then he climbed into the boat with them, and the wind died down. (Mark 6:48–51)

The Hebrews believed Sheol (or hell) was in the deepest parts of the earth and there were doorways to hell in the sea.[2] That's why they were scared. They thought Jesus was a ghost from hell. They fell for the superstitions of false religions.

Mark's version of the story gives us a compelling story of Jesus' power, but not all the details of this story are included in Mark's version. John's version adds some details:

> They had rowed three or four miles when suddenly they saw Jesus walking on the water toward the boat. They were terrified, but he called out to them, "Don't be afraid. I am here!" Then they were eager to let him in the boat, and immediately they arrived at their destination! (John 6:19–21)

John's version of the story is missing something too. Did you catch it? Where is Peter in this story? Neither Mark nor John thought Peter walking on the water was worth reporting. Apparently, this story is about more than Peter walking on the water. In fact, many scholars think Peter wrote a part of Mark's book. If that's true, even Peter left Peter out of the story. However, Matthew's version of the story does include the detail about Peter:

---

1. Ortberg, *If You Want to Walk on Water*.
2. Richter, "11 Hidden Spots."

> When the disciples saw him walking on the water, they were terrified. In their fear, they cried out, "It's a ghost!" But Jesus spoke to them at once. "Don't be afraid," he said. "Take courage. I am here!" Then Peter called to him, "Lord, if it's really you, tell me to come to you, walking on the water." "Yes, come," Jesus said. So Peter went over the side of the boat and walked on the water toward Jesus. But when he saw the strong wind and the waves, he was terrified and began to sink. "Save me, Lord!" he shouted. Jesus immediately reached out and grabbed him. "You have so little faith," Jesus said. "Why did you doubt me?" When they climbed back into the boat, the wind stopped. (Matt 14:25–32)

We translate this Greek word *phantasma* as ghost[3] because we don't have another word that truly conveys their folklore. They thought Jesus was a sea monster from hell,[4] but Peter was the only one brave enough to investigate. He might also have been motivated by keeping the sea creature in the water and away from the other disciples, but this isn't about getting out of a boat. This story is about trusting Jesus enough to let him in the boat. There's a lot of us who are too scared to let Jesus into our lives because we don't know what he'll do when he gets in, but his presence makes all the difference. It's great to walk on water, but the wind didn't stop until Jesus got into the boat. Peter, in his doubt, walked on water, but when the doubt was gone, Jesus got in the boat. The storm stopped when Jesus came in.

Growing up, my dad would never let anyone else in the family drive his car. If dad was in the car, he was driving. When we let Jesus in the boat, he steers. When we receive Christ into our lives, we make him Lord of our lives. His priorities become our priorities. His values become our values. His heart becomes our heart. Let him in.

When we let Jesus come into our lives, he calms the storm. When he comes in, he might make us change things. He'll do some cleaning and fixing, but he makes us better. He will calm the storm, and he will calm us.

No political party or American dream can do that. A hobby can't do that. Power can't do that, and wealth can't do that. In fact, as wealth grows, it eventually brings misery. At some point, wealth causes more storms than it calms.

If you give God control of your life, he will make your life better, and he will make you better at life. He will give you true joy. Don't look for something in creation to define you. Look to the Creator.

3. Bible Hub, "Strong's Greek: 5326. φάντασμα (phantasma)."
4. Steinmeyer, "Biblical Monsters."

Before we can change the minds of people, we have to change their hearts. Before we can change their hearts, we have to change our hearts. When the Christian church in America rejected Christ's way of neighboring and traded it for a rule of the "moral majority," we doomed ourselves to the problems we are currently facing. We are eerily like the nation Jesus lived in, and we need to again hear his words of reprimand.

The Moral Majority was a political organization in the 1980s that was led by Christians who made deals with devils. Who were those devils? Politicians. "Devil" means "deceiver," and deception is the dominant tool of politics. The Moral Majority agreed to support fiscal policies of greed if the politicians would support hatred for the sins that were popular to hate at the time.

We are only able to call ourselves the moral majority because we dumb down our morality. We elevate the sins of outsiders and excuse our pride, gluttony, hatred, and selfishness. Our go-to sins are the sins Jesus pointed out most. Our hearts must change lest the enemy comes to destroy our temples, and this time the temple isn't a building in Jerusalem. It's us.

As we attempt to understand scripture in pursuit of right living, we choose not to point to morality but to Jesus. Our goal is not to make the world more moral. Our goal is to make the world more saved. Our goal is not to become more independent, but to become more dependent on Jesus. Our goal is not to become more politically free, but to become more spiritually free.

Reflect: What storm in your life can only God calm, and how can you more fully surrender it to him?

28

Storm the Gates of Hell

Accompanying Scripture Reading: Matthew 16:5–18

ONE DAY JESUS TOOK his disciples to a place in Caesarea Philippi where sexual immorality was prominently displayed. Caesarea Philippi was a city built for one primary purpose, to worship the gods. They built the city on a giant rock at the entrance to a large cave from which water flowed and served as a tributary of the Jordan River. Many people at the time believed that cave was a portal to hell.[1] They called the cave "the gate of hell." For them, hell wasn't a place of fire. It was a damp, dark cave.

The primary god that was worshiped at Caesarea Philippi was Baal. Then, in 300 to 200 BC, the Greeks made it a temple for the Greek god Pan, the god of fertility. That is when they stopped calling it Caesarea Philippi and started calling it Panius (or Banius), and the Romans built Banius into

1. Vander Laan, "Gates of Hell."

a large city. There was a temple for Augustus, a court for worshiping Pan, the Temple of Zeus, and the temples of the dancing goats. They set up female statues with which they believed the god Pan would come down in the winter to copulate. Then, he would descend into the cave to hell. When he ascended from hell, he would go to the heavens and rain down fertility on their crops. Rain was believed to be Pan's semen fertilizing the land and the women in spring.

The Pan statue was half goat and half man with large genitals and a flute. Worshiping him involved drinking large quantities of alcohol, doing drugs, and playing loud music. The priests and worshipers would force the goats to mate. Then they would all join in, in detestable ways. It was Pandemonium, but it gets worse. To appease the gods, they threw babies into the water in the cave to sacrifice them to the gods.[2]

This is where Jesus brought his disciples, and they didn't go there because it was on the way to another location. It was thirty miles north of the Sea of Galilee, and it was completely forbidden for Jews to go there. To put this action into perspective, Tiberius (the capital city of the region) was only a few miles south of where Jesus lived, and we don't have any record of Jesus going there. Jesus was uninterested in political interactions. He told people to "give to Caesar what is Caesar's" (Matt 22:21) because he wasn't interested in politics. He had a bigger fight to wage. His battle wasn't against flesh and blood. It was against the rulers of hell.

It was in Caesarea Philippi that Jesus asked his disciples to confess who he is, and Peter's answer to that question can give us some insight into why Jesus picked Peter to lead his disciples and to lead the Christian church. Peter regularly screwed up, but he followed God:

> When Jesus came to the region of Caesarea Philippi, he asked his disciples, "Who do people say that the Son of Man is?" "Well," they replied, "some say John the Baptist, some say Elijah, and others say Jeremiah or one of the other prophets." Then he asked them, "But who do you say I am?" Simon Peter answered, "You are the Messiah, the Son of the living God." Jesus replied, "You are blessed, Simon son of John, because my Father in heaven has revealed this to you. You did not learn this from any human being. Now I say to you that you are Peter (which means 'rock'), and upon this rock I will build my church, and all the powers of hell will not conquer it." (Matt 16:13–19)

2. Caesarea Philippi and pagan worship: Daley, "Ancient Greeks"; Elder, "Caesarea Philippi"; Fisher, "Bestiality"; Vander Laan, "Fertility Cults" and "Gates of Hell."

THE LIFE

Unfortunately, the translators added a parenthetical comment about the definition of Peter's name, but the comment is somewhat misleading. The Greek word for "Peter" is *Petros* which does mean "rock," but usually it's referring to a small rock.[3] Jesus didn't say, "Upon this '*petros*.'" He said, "Upon this '*petra*.'" *Petra* usually refers to a large rock or a boulder.[4] Jesus was metaphorically talking about a few rocks: he was talking about the foundational rock that Peter had just talked about, that Jesus is the Messiah. He was talking about Peter and the church. And he was talking about the rock on which Caesarea Philippi is built.

There is also another unfortunate translation in this passage. The NLT uses the phrase "the powers of hell," but the correct translation of the Greek *pulé* is "gate."[5] Jesus and his disciples were standing at the gates of hell, on a rock. This is not about God protecting us when the satan attacks. Gates don't attack. Gates defend. In Jesus' scenario, we are on offense. We wage the war, and hell doesn't stand a chance. I grew up with the ignorant idea that Christianity is declining, but that is a lie of the satan. The church isn't losing. We are on offense, and we will win!

Jesus did not teach his disciples to retreat from the sinful society. He taught them to storm the gates of hell. He doesn't want us cowering in fear of physical pain or persecution. The common habit of bunkering and prepping for disaster cannot be justified with Scripture. Those practices are historically naïve, strategically ineffective, and selfishly sinful.

If we are going to fulfill God's Great Commission in the spirit of the Great Commandment, we must take intentional steps to interact with people who are far from God. Jesus taught his followers to be a light:

> You are the light of the world—like a city on a hilltop that cannot be hidden. (Matt 5:14)

Reflect: In what ways have you joined the front lines of the Christian mission to seek and save the lost?

---

3. Bible Hub, "Strong's Greek: 4074. Πέτρος (Petros)."
4. Bible Hub, "Strong's Greek: 4073. πέτρα (petra)."
5. Bible Hub, "Strong's Greek: 4439. πύλη (pulé)." This difference is also pointed out in footnote b of Matt 16:18 NLT.

29

Be a Rock

Accompanying Scripture Reading: Matthew 16:13–23

PETER IS OFTEN VIEWED as the leader of the apostles. He regularly risked his life for the Christian mission; that is, until he understood the Christian mission involved the death of Jesus. As Jesus marched to his crucifixion, three times Peter denied that he was a follower of Christ. Peter defended Jesus when he believed he was going to establish an earthly kingdom. However, he was ashamed of Jesus when he discovered God's kingdom was actually a spiritual kingdom. Peter didn't want to serve a crucified king. He wanted to rule with a military commander, a political leader. When Peter betrayed Jesus, he assumed they had lost. Why would he remain faithful to a dead movement?

Most leaders would see Peter's betrayal as disqualification for future leadership, but that is not how Jesus responded. Most leaders recognize that putting this kind of person in a leadership position is an unwise, risky decision. Even so, Jesus chose Peter to lead the Christian church. Could Jesus see the future? Or did he simply choose to trust Peter, knowing his heart? Peter needed to renew his mind, to think of heaven instead of earth. Jesus recognized Peter's teachable spirit and was patient through that process.

Matthew 16 describes a time that Jesus took his disciples to a place of extreme immorality, Caesarea Philippi. While they were there, Jesus asked his followers, "Who do you think I am," and as usual, Peter was the first to respond:

> Simon Peter answered, "You are the Messiah, the Son of the living God." Jesus replied, "You are blessed, Simon son of John, because my Father in heaven has revealed this to you. You did not learn this from any human being." (Matt 16:16–17)

Verse 17 reveals part of the reason Jesus chose Peter to lead the Christian church. Peter listened to God. He was open to hearing from and being led by the Spirit. He didn't have all the answers, but he was willing to learn. He regularly failed, but he followed God. When Jesus called Peter "blessed," he knew Peter would deny him.

When Jesus saved you, he knew you would screw up, and he saved you anyway. God uses screwed up people to lead his church. Welcome to the team.

> On the way, Jesus told them, "Tonight all of you will desert me. For the Scriptures say, 'God will strike the Shepherd, and the sheep of the flock will be scattered.' But after I have been raised from the dead, I will go ahead of you to Galilee and meet you there." Peter declared, "Even if everyone else deserts you, I will never desert you." Jesus replied, "I tell you the truth, Peter—this very night, before the rooster crows, you will deny three times that you even know me." "No!" Peter insisted. "Even if I have to die with you, I will never deny you!" And all the other disciples vowed the same. (Matt 26:31–35)

Jesus knew Peter would betray him, but he also knew what Peter would do after he denied knowing Jesus. After the rooster crowed three times, Peter was overwhelmed with regret:

> Peter left the courtyard, weeping bitterly. (Luke 22:62)

When you feel guilt, thank God for that feeling. It reveals that the Holy Spirit is active in your life. It reveals that your heart has not become calloused. Feelings of guilt are evidence that your heart is alive, not spiritually dead.

After Peter did what he said he would never do, he was broken. Until he had an encounter with Jesus, who was cooking breakfast on a beach after the resurrection, Peter likely experienced extreme regret. While they were eating breakfast on the beach that morning, Jesus asked Peter a question similar to the question he asked when they were at Caesarea Philippi. Three times Jesus asked Peter about his heart. Jesus asked him, "Peter, do you love me?" And three times Peter replied, "Yes." And three times, Jesus asked Peter to lead the church, to feed his sheep:

> A third time [Jesus] asked him, "Simon son of John, do you love me?" Peter was hurt that Jesus asked the question a third time. He said, "Lord, you know everything. You know that I love you." Jesus said, "Then feed my sheep." (John 21:17)

Jesus gave Peter a chance to repent three times, one for each betrayal. Peter renewed his mind. He traded his shame for faith. This set Peter up to become the great leader of the church that we know he was.

We see Peter again in the book of Acts preaching boldly about his faith in Jesus:

> Peter replied, "Each of you must repent of your sins and turn to God, and be baptized in the name of Jesus Christ for the forgiveness of your sins." . . . Those who believed what Peter said were baptized and added to the church that day—about 3,000 in all. (Acts 2:38, 41)

Recognize that Peter was inviting people to repent, to change their minds, to stop seeing the world from a worldly perspective, and to begin seeing the world from a heavenly perspective. And how many people were baptized? Three thousand: one thousand people for every betrayal, one thousand people for every confession.

By this time, Peter had reached a new level of faith. Peter had now accepted the fact that Jesus' kingdom was an eternal kingdom, a heavenly kingdom. He was ready to give up his life in this world because he recognized his true home in heaven. Eventually, Peter was killed for his faith. They crucified him upside down.

When someone challenges your faith in Jesus, will you deny him or profess your undying loyalty to him?

I am not ashamed of this Good News about Christ. (Rom 1:16)

Reflect: Does your citizenship in heaven take precedence over earthly kingdoms, and is your faith in Jesus central to your identity or just a small part of your life?

30

Don't Be a Satan

Accompanying Scripture Reading: Matthew 16:21–28

THERE WERE MANY TIMES that Jesus told people not to tell others about things he had said and done. It appears he did this for multiple reasons. One reason was that he was not yet ready to make his ministry public. Jesus knew that announcing who he was would begin his journey to the cross. The bloody sweat in the Garden of Gethsemane is evidence that Jesus was dreading that journey. In fact, Jesus asked God to find a way to redeem the world that did not involve him being tortured and killed on a cross. But eventually, Jesus did go public. And when he began that journey, he walked into the inevitable attacks of the enemy:

> From then on Jesus began to tell his disciples plainly that it was necessary for him to go to Jerusalem, and that he would suffer many terrible things at the hands of the elders, the leading priests,

and the teachers of religious law. He would be killed, but on the third day he would be raised from the dead. But Peter took him aside and began to reprimand him for saying such things. "Heaven forbid, Lord," he said. "This will never happen to you!" Jesus turned to Peter and said, "Get away from me, Satan! You are a dangerous trap to me. You are seeing things merely from a human point of view, not from God's." (Matt 16:21–23)

When Peter argued with Jesus' description of the salvation plan, Jesus called him a "satan," which means "tempter" or "deceiver." The translators of the Bible are in the habit of using the word "satan" as a name for the primary adversary of the Bible, but that is not his name. That is a description of who he is, but this satan, "the satan," is not simply "a satan." He is "the satan," the primary villain, the opposer of goodness. We can all be "a satan," but there is only one "the satan."

In Matt 16, Jesus was not implying Peter was the supreme adversary. He was telling Peter to stop tempting him. Peter tempted Jesus to not do what Jesus was called to do.

We are often tempted to reject God's plan when we think our plan is better. Jesus' invitation to pick up our crosses was an invitation to follow God's plan instead of our own. Our way, no matter how benevolent or moral we believe it is, will only lead to destruction.

When we sin, or when we tempt others to sin, we are a satan. When hell breaks loose, it's because humans let it break loose. Adam and Eve did it first, and we keep the tradition going. Some of our pain is caused by our sin. Some of our pain is caused by the sins of people around us, but all pain is caused by sin. In other words, when we resist the satan and his sinful temptations, we decrease pain in the world.

Our primary temptation is to believe our plan and our ideas are better than God's plan. This is how the satan tricked Adam and Eve into eating the fruit. He convinced them God's instructions were flawed or incomplete. The satan convinced Adam and Eve they could be like God rather than follow God.

Churches add rules to Scripture believing our experience and sociological research are superior to biblical truth. This is how churches end up with rules like: no dancing, no drinking caffeine, no drinking alcohol, no movies, no smoking, no hats in the auditorium, etc. Our membership rules would keep Jesus from being a member of our church. You won't find these rules in Scripture, but apparently, we believe we know better than Scripture:

> You have died with Christ, and he has set you free from the spiritual powers of this world. So why do you keep on following the rules of the world, such as, "Don't handle! Don't taste! Don't touch!"? Such rules are mere human teachings about things that deteriorate as we use them. These rules may seem wise because they require strong devotion, pious self-denial, and severe bodily discipline. But they provide no help in conquering a person's evil desires. (Col 2:20–23)

The apostle Paul told us that pious self-denial doesn't help us conquer evil desires. Maybe our legalism isn't as helpful as we think it is. Maybe God's way of freedom and grace is best:

> "My thoughts are nothing like your thoughts," says the Lord. "And my ways are far beyond anything you could imagine. For just as the heavens are higher than the earth, so my ways are higher than your ways and my thoughts higher than your thoughts." (Isa 55:8–9)

Another great temptation is to prioritize the pursuit of wealth, fame, or power. This is what causes politics to play a major role in our church gatherings. We blur the lines between citizenship in our government and citizenship in God's kingdom, and we use this logic to justify disunity. The prosperity gospel teaches us to give ourselves to these things, to fight for them, and to expect to have them, but Jesus never got distracted by these things. He fought real evil, not political battles.

Jesus surprised the Pharisees when he told them to "give to Caesar what belongs to Caesar" (Matt 22:21) rather than fight the political battle. Jesus operated on a divine timetable, guided by his Father's will rather than human expectations. This offers a valuable lesson for us today. There are times when God's plan may not align with our desires or our priorities, and it can be challenging to accept this.

Think about times in your life when you've felt an inclination towards a certain path, only to encounter obstacles or a sense of divine redirection. Perhaps you were passionate about a career, relationship, or project, but circumstances seemed to steer you away. In those moments it's natural to feel frustrated or disappointed. However, these instances can also be opportunities to trust that God has a greater plan in mind, one that is ultimately for our good, even if it's not immediately apparent:

> Trust in the Lord with all your heart; do not depend on your own understanding. Seek his will in all you do, and he will show you which path to take. (Prov 3:5–6)

Here are six steps you can take to follow God's way rather than your own:

- Prayer and Surrender: Begin with prayer, asking God to reveal his will to you. Be open to whatever direction God may provide, even if it differs from your desires.

- Seek Wisdom in Scripture: The Bible is a foundational tool for understanding God's will. Regularly reading and meditating on Scripture helps us learn God's character and commands.

- Consult Wise Counsel: Seeking advice from trusted spiritual mentors, pastors, or mature Christian friends can provide clarity. These individuals can offer a different perspective and help confirm what you believe God is leading you to do.

- Observe Circumstances: While not all circumstances are signs from God, paying attention to the doors God opens or closes can provide insight into his will. If a particular opportunity consistently faces obstacles, it might be worth reevaluating if it aligns with God's plan for you.

- Listen to the Holy Spirit: The Holy Spirit can and will guide us. Cultivating a habit of listening to the Spirit's guidance can help us stay aligned with God's will.

- Practice Patience and Trust: God's timing is perfect, and sometimes we need to wait for his plan to unfold. Trust that God sees the bigger picture and knows what is best for you.

When we let go of our need for control and embrace his guidance, we open ourselves to a life of purpose and fulfillment that aligns with his divine will. As you go forward, reflect on the areas where you might be resisting God's plan. Ask for the strength to follow his lead, even when it challenges your comfort or desires. In doing so, you align yourself with the ultimate example of obedience and trust—Jesus Christ.

We resist the satan by running to God, by following his way. We must know what tempts us so we can run from it. Coming close to God is practical. He laid out his plan for us. Humble yourself and follow his instructions. Even though Jesus did not want to go to the cross, he did it anyway. He did it because he loves you and because he trusted his Father's plan.

Reflect: Which of the six steps in following God's way do you find most challenging?

31

His Glory and Grace

Accompanying Scripture Reading: Matthew 17:1–20

MOSES IS A GREAT hero of the Jewish and Christian faiths because of his ability, through the power of God, to deliver the Israelites from slavery in Egypt. He lived a long life and eventually died at Mount Nebo, in the wilderness of Jordan. Although Moses was a great man of faith, he wasn't good enough. His incredible actions were not enough to make up for even small sins. For that reason, God told Moses he would not be allowed to enter the promised land of Israel:

> You failed to demonstrate my holiness to the people of Israel there.
> So you will see the land from a distance, but you may not enter the
> land I am giving to the people of Israel. (Deut 32:51–52)

We are tempted to believe that our good behavior makes up for our bad behavior, but that is not how God works. If that were the case, then

Moses' good works would have easily made up for his bad behavior. The solution to bad behavior is not good behavior. The only solution to bad behavior is punishment. Our sins require punishment. In fact, our sins require death. The good news for us is that Jesus took that punishment for us, but Moses lived before Jesus died on the cross for our sins.

I assume that as Moses was dying, he was positive that his fate was sealed and that his sin was going to keep him from his hopes and dreams.

Growing up in the church, I regularly heard that Moses was not allowed to enter the promised land because he sinned in the wilderness, but that's not the full story. When Jesus was on earth, he had an experience that transformed him. We call this experience The Transfiguration:

> Jesus took Peter and the two brothers, James and John, and led them up a high mountain to be alone. As the men watched, Jesus' appearance was transformed so that his face shone like the sun, and his clothes became as white as light. Suddenly, Moses and Elijah appeared and began talking with Jesus. (Matt 17:1–3)

This event did not take place on Mount Nebo. It happened on one of the mountains in Galilee, in Israel. More importantly, it was in the promised land of Israel. Because of Jesus' glory and grace, Moses was forgiven, and he did enter the promised land.

If you think your sins have disqualified you, they haven't. Because of Jesus' glory and grace, you can be forgiven! Moses did get to enter the promised land, and you will too.

Our promised land is heaven. It is the promised inheritance of everyone who has put their faith in Jesus Christ. It is not a reward for people who commit fewer than a set number of sins, and it is not a reward for good behavior. It is a gift for those who will receive it.

> Then I saw a new heaven and a new earth, for the old heaven and the old earth had disappeared. And the sea was also gone. And I saw the holy city, the new Jerusalem, coming down from God out of heaven like a bride beautifully dressed for her husband. I heard a loud shout from the throne, saying, "Look, God's home is now among his people! He will live with them, and they will be his people. God himself will be with them. He will wipe every tear from their eyes, and there will be no more death or sorrow or crying or pain. All these things are gone forever." (Rev 21:1–4)

Elijah, another great hero of the faith, was also on the mountain when Jesus was transfigured. That leaves us to wonder why God chose these two men to be present in this moment. For that answer, let's look at the significance of these two figures. Moses was the giver of the law, and Elijah was one of Israel's most significant prophets. The law and the prophets were the foundation of the old covenant that God gave to the Israelites. The transfiguration shows Jesus had not come to reject the law and the prophets. Jesus came to fulfill the law and the prophets.

The Jewish religious leaders hated Jesus because he claimed to be their promised Messiah, but they also hated Jesus because he preached a gospel that was contrary to the law of Moses. Jesus was establishing a new covenant that did not follow the Jewish traditions, and the Jewish leaders would eventually kill him because of it.

The transfiguration occurred just days after the first time Jesus predicted to his disciples that he was going to die. It seems that because of this prediction, his disciples had begun to doubt whether he truly was the Messiah. Even though they had seen and performed many miracles, the faith of Jesus' disciples, like the faith of the Israelites in the wilderness, was shaky. In fact, as Peter, James, John, and Jesus returned from the mountain of the transfiguration, they reunited with the other disciples to discover them struggling to drive a demon out of a man. When they asked why they couldn't get the job done, Jesus blamed their lack of faith:

> Afterward the disciples asked Jesus privately, "Why couldn't we cast out that demon?" "You don't have enough faith," Jesus told them. (Matt 17:19–20)

When the apostles began to doubt Jesus, the transfiguration served as a reminder of Christ's deity, of his glory and grace. Let it do the same for you. The events of the life of Christ give plenty of affirmation of his glory. God the Father and the Holy Spirit affirmed Jesus at his baptism. Jesus was empowered to perform miracles. Moses and Elijah affirmed Jesus at the transfiguration. Jesus rose from the dead. He is who he says he is. Put your faith in him.

Reflect: Do you ever struggle to accept God's forgiveness and trust God for your salvation?

32

Give Attention

Accompanying Scripture Reading: Matthew 18:1–14

SELFISHNESS IS OUR DEFAULT attitude. When a baby is born, she focuses all her attention on her needs. She is as needy as a person can be. She is completely reliant on the love of someone else for her health and safety. However, as she experiences the love of others, she learns the utility of love. She matures as she recognizes the benefits of the love that is given to her, and she learns to love.

Unless there is something wrong with us, we eventually become less needy than we were when we were children. Unless we allow ourselves to be overcome by some harmful addiction, we learn to work hard to provide for ourselves. We feed and clothe ourselves. We protect ourselves, accumulate accolades, seek pleasure, and fight for promotion. Even if we are not satisfied with ourselves, we love ourselves immensely. That is why Jesus tells us to love others as much as we love ourselves. That's a lot of love.

Give Attention

Love your neighbor as yourself. (Mark 12:31)

We naturally focus the majority of our attention on ourselves, but true love gives attention to others. We buy attention from servers at restaurants, from entertainers, and from babysitters. We pay employees to tend to our needs and help us pursue our goals. There is nothing wrong with this kind of attention, but this kind of attention cannot be described as love. As demonstrated in the temptation to pay for sex, loving attention is given, not paid for. That is why sex is meant to be contained within the fellowship of a committed relationship.

The lack of love in our world has led people to seek attention through claiming victimhood, dressing provocatively, and screaming for attention like a newborn baby. The common habit of young people in our world to gather to protest, strike, and riot is a cry for attention. It is often a demonstration of immaturity and self-focus, but occasionally it is an act of selfless love, of defending those who cannot defend themselves.

As Christians, we seek to give unearned attention to hurting people like a mother gives attention to her newborn daughter. My children did nothing to earn my love. I gave it to them enthusiastically before they were even born, and anything short of that would have been sinful neglect. I cannot imagine a more terrifying evil than a parent who intentionally harms his own child. That blatantly goes against God's created order.

Plato asked us to consider if something is good because God commands it, or does God command it because it is good.[1] The answer is "yes" to both options. God created the world with miraculous order and called it good, and for God's creation to work properly, people must continually mature to become sacrificially loving.

The love of our world is not love at all. It is passion, emotion, and temporary satisfaction. True love is spiritual love. It is fulfilling, uplifting, and eternal. True love requires maturity, and as we mature spiritually, we learn to give attention to those who need to experience spiritual love.

In fact, the most mature Christians are those who have made loving people who need to be loved a top priority. They don't wait for people to ask for love, then begrudgingly give it. They seek out people who have not experienced the sacrificial love of mature Christian faith. Jesus told many parables about giving attention to people who need love. Here is one:

---

1. Plato, *Euthyphro*.

> If a man has a hundred sheep and one of them wanders away, what will he do? Won't he leave the ninety-nine others on the hills and go out to search for the one that is lost? And if he finds it, I tell you the truth, he will rejoice over it more than over the ninety-nine that didn't wander away! In the same way, it is not my heavenly Father's will that even one of these little ones should perish. (Matt 18:12–14)

There is no greater pain than the pain of distance from God. That is hell. You can numb that pain with the temporary pleasures of this world, but those things can only lead to dissatisfaction and depression.

As we look around our world and see people who are lost without eternal hope, it should motivate us to get out of our comfort zones, adjust priorities, and make sacrifices so that lost people can experience and benefit from the eternal love of God.

The Christian church is relentlessly tempted to become inwardly focused. In the stories of the prodigal son (Luke 15:11–32) and the lost sheep, Jesus demonstrates the importance of giving attention to lost people rather than focusing on ourselves.

Some sheep are lost intentionally. They ran from their shepherd to pursue something appealing on a different path. Some sheep are lost by accident. They got separated from the herd in a storm or when a predator attacked. Our world is full of lost sheep of both kinds.

The shepherd found more joy in finding the lost sheep because it was lost, not because the sheep was more beautiful or healthy. The shepherd's love is generous and unearned. The sheep who remain with the herd experience the fellowship and protection of the herd, but without that protection the lost sheep's time is short. The shepherd is motivated to bring the lost sheep into the fold so that it can grow into maturity.

Do you give attention to lost people who have not earned your love? Spend some time thinking about the people in your community that need to experience the unconditional love of Jesus. Pray for them, but don't stop there. Do what the shepherd did. Go serve them. Give them attention.

Reflect: What habits help you remember to give unearned love and care to those who are hurting?

33

The Lies We Feel

Accompanying Scripture Reading: John 8:31–51

JESUS FOCUSED ON ONE sin more than any other, the sin of pride. Jesus invites us to humble ourselves before God and receive his gift of grace rather than working to achieve salvation through our own goodness to bolster our pride. Jesus surrounded himself with people who recognized their need for a savior rather than portraying themselves as righteous saviors. Because of this, the self-righteous religious leaders in Jesus' day often found themselves at odds with Jesus.

In John 8, Jesus had an encounter with some religious leaders who were bragging about their ancestry and authority. Jesus invited them to follow him, but these religious leaders were uninterested in following. They wanted to be followed. They were deaf to the truth because the volume of their pride was so high. The religious leaders bragged about being children of Abraham, but Jesus called them children of the devil:

> Why can't you understand what I am saying? It's because you can't even hear me! For you are the children of your father the devil, and you love to do the evil things he does. He was a murderer from the beginning. He has always hated the truth, because there is no truth in him. When he lies, it is consistent with his character; for he is a liar and the father of lies. (John 8:43–44)

The snake deceived Eve in the garden, and he has deceived vulnerable people ever since. What lie does the satan tell you? Does he tell you that you need to work harder to earn God's love? Does he tell you that your sins are too bad, that you can't be forgiven? Does he tell you that you don't need God, that you can make it on your own? The satan is a liar, but Jesus is the truth.

The satan's agenda is destruction. Jesus did not portray the satan as an idea, but as a being. This being is the father of lies. The satan wants to kill you because he hates your Father. Like a virus attacks a computer, the satan attacks our faith. He wants to kill our bodies, but he would prefer to deceive us and lead us away from God.

The satan's method is deception. He can't physically touch us, but he can use deception to get us to inflict pain on ourselves. He attempts to convince us that God does not love us, that our sins disqualify us, or that our goodness qualifies us.

The satan's fruit are fear, sadness, doubt, conspiracy, insecurity, jealousy, pride, and selfishness. If these words describe your life, you are not a joyful person. The satan has stolen God's joy from you to weaken you, because God's joy is your strength. The fruits of the satan are emotions because these emotions make us vulnerable to manipulation.

Emotions are an invisible force on our actions. Good emotions can lead to good actions. Because I love my sons, I choose to sacrifice for them. We often do what we do because of the emotions that motivate us, but we must learn to not trust our emotions. Instead, we are invited to trust the truth of Jesus Christ. The joy of the Lord is our strength because joy is not an emotion. Joy is a state of mind that results from a healthy relationship with the truth.

For this reason, it is healthy to periodically take an inventory of our emotions. Physiologically, there are complex chemical reactions in our bodies that make it difficult to remain focused on truth. Doctors can balance chemicals to assist with these struggles, but the problem is never fully solved. Socially, there are distractions in the world that cause painful emotions. Counselors can help us wrestle with the relational pain we experience, but new pains will be inflicted. Spiritually, battles are being fought all around us that impact our physical reality, and the only way to withstand these attacks is by moving closer to God.

If you will draw close to God, the Holy Spirit will give you peace as you trust in him. You were separated from God by a giant river that you couldn't cross. So, God built a bridge so that you can live with him:

> But the Holy Spirit produces this kind of fruit in our lives: love, joy, peace, patience, kindness, goodness, faithfulness, gentleness, and self-control. There is no law against these things! Those who belong to Christ Jesus have nailed the passions and desires of their sinful nature to his cross and crucified them there. Since we are living by the Spirit, let us follow the Spirit's leading in every part of our lives. Let us not become conceited, or provoke one another, or be jealous of one another. (Gal 5:22–26)

The fruits of the Holy Spirit are not emotions. They are actions. When we move closer to God, healthy actions result. He helps us to become the people he created us to be and to do the things he created us to do:

> Resist the devil, and he will flee from you. Come close to God, and God will come close to you. (Jas 4:7–8)

We cannot resist the devil alone. His lies are too persuasive. Our only hope is a relationship with the Holy Spirit. Come close to God. Humble yourself before him and trust his truth rather than your emotions. Supernatural progress is made when we draw near to God. Relentless joy is available to all of God's children because he is with us:

> The Lord is close to the brokenhearted; he rescues those whose spirits are crushed. (Ps 34:18)

It is God who does the rescuing. We cannot save ourselves. Without God, we cannot eternally fix our problems. Without God, we are dead in our sins, and dead people cannot save themselves. We need God to raise us from the dead, to give us a new life, so that we can live the life he created us to live.

Reflect: After taking an inventory of your emotions, which ones tend to hold you back from doing the actions God created you to do?

34

Open Your Doors

Accompanying Scripture Reading: Luke 16:19–31

Penn Jillette, the famous magician, once recorded a video criticizing Christians who do not proselytize.[1] The video went viral, and the reason so many people watched it was because Penn Jillette is an outspoken atheist. Why would an atheist criticize Christians who don't try to convince him and other atheists that they should believe in God? He said it this way, "How much do you have to hate somebody to believe everlasting life is possible and not tell them that? I mean, if I believed, beyond the shadow of a doubt, that a truck was coming at you, and you didn't believe that truck was bearing down on you, there is a certain point where I tackle you. And this is more important than that."

---

1. Jillette, "Gift of a Bible."

I believe it is our responsibility to win people to Christ, but so few Christians have a plan to take the gospel message to the lost people around them:

> Work at telling others the Good News, and fully carry out the ministry God has given you. (2 Tim 4:5)

The apostle Paul told Timothy that God gave Timothy a mission to tell people about Jesus, and the apostle Paul would say the same thing to you. Make a plan. Find a way to share the love of God with people in need.

In Luke 16, Luke records a story that Jesus told about a rich guy and a poor guy:

> Jesus said, "There was a certain rich man who was splendidly clothed in purple and fine linen and who lived each day in luxury. At his gate lay a poor man named Lazarus who was covered with sores. As Lazarus lay there longing for scraps from the rich man's table, the dogs would come and lick his open sores." (Luke 16:19–21)

This is not a true story. It's a parable. Jesus created this story to teach a lesson. In his created story, Jesus put purple clothes on the rich man. In other words, Jesus wants you to picture royalty or the richest person you can think of. Think of Elon Musk, and on Musk's front porch, picture a homeless man who is covered in oozing sores. If Jesus described a man with oozing sores in the first century, he was likely describing a man with leprosy. The fact that the sores were oozing implies that this was an advanced case of leprosy. This poor man was a contagious leper. We then have to ask ourselves, "Why would Elon Musk allow a homeless guy with contagious leprosy to live on his porch?" Apparently, he is a very generous rich guy. In fact, Lazarus was on Elon Musk's front porch long enough to build a relationship with the guard dogs who were licking his sores.

This story is a *hapax legomenon*. It is the only fictional story Jesus told in which Jesus named a character. Because Jesus didn't use arbitrary details in his stories, we must assume Jesus gave the poor man the name Lazarus for a reason. If I made up a story about two people and named one of the characters Darci, my wife's name, you would assume that character in the story is incredibly intelligent, attractive, and kind (I just earned some brownie points). And if I called the other person in the story "an ugly guy," you could easily interpret what I was trying to imply about these two fictional characters. "Lazarus" was the name of one of Jesus' closest friends.

Therefore, Jesus gave honor to this fictional character by giving him the name "Lazarus."

Simply allowing Lazarus to stay on this porch violated the laws of Judaism. Jews in this time were required to separate themselves from lepers, to keep themselves clean. As Elon Musk's rich friends were coming and going from his house, they likely asked him, "Why do you let this disgusting man stay here? He's getting us sick. Get him out of here." Leprosy was a deadly disease, and eventually it killed the poor man:

> Finally, the poor man died and was carried by the angels to sit beside Abraham at the heavenly banquet. The rich man also died and was buried, and he went to the place of the dead. There, in torment, he saw Abraham in the far distance with Lazarus at his side. The rich man shouted, "Father Abraham, have some pity! Send Lazarus over here to dip the tip of his finger in water and cool my tongue. I am in anguish in these flames." But Abraham said to him, "Son, remember that during your lifetime you had everything you wanted, and Lazarus had nothing. So now he is here being comforted, and you are in anguish. And besides, there is a great chasm separating us. No one can cross over to you from here, and no one can cross over to us from there." Then the rich man said, "Please, Father Abraham, at least send him to my father's home. For I have five brothers, and I want him to warn them so they don't end up in this place of torment." (Luke 16:22–28)

When Jesus, in his made-up story, put the rich man in hell and the poor man in heaven, he likely caught everyone off guard. They would have assumed the rich man would go to heaven, and the poor would go to hell. They would have been tempted to believe the leprosy was evidence Lazarus had been rejected by God, but Jesus switched the expected roles. Now the rich guy has lost control, and he is begging Lazarus for a drop of water.

On earth, the poor guy was an outcast. Apparently, even his family had abandoned him. But, in heaven, Lazarus was in the place of honor at Abraham's side.

The rich man expected to find a way to purchase freedom from hell, to use his power to get ahead, but the wealth of this world has no power in eternity. When we enter eternity, there aren't any second chances. Indulgences don't work. When we die, we face a final judgment. Now Elon has an eternal perspective. He realizes his money on earth did nothing.

Another detail Jesus inserted into this story is the number of brothers the rich man had. Why did he include this detail? We don't have specifics about other details of the story. We don't know how many guard dogs there were. I think Jesus was trying to show us that the rich man thought he had five brothers, but he really had six. Rich and powerful people were often the villains in Jesus' stories, and this time, even though Jesus gave a generous description of the rich man, the rich man was still the villain. Why? The rich man was the villain because he failed to see the outcast as his brother.

This story is meant to teach us to open our doors to outcasts. It's not enough to throw them the scraps from our table. We're tempted to preach truth to people as long as they keep their distance, but Jesus wants us to develop a plan to take the good news of God's love to them. We are to be like Jesus, and Jesus didn't simply heal lepers from a distance. Jesus touched lepers.

This is how we should reach lost people. We invite people to come as they are. We reach out with radical love and generosity.

> But Abraham said, "Moses and the prophets have warned them. Your brothers can read what they wrote." The rich man replied, "No, Father Abraham! But if someone is sent to them from the dead, then they will repent of their sins and turn to God." But Abraham said, "If they won't listen to Moses and the prophets, they won't be persuaded even if someone rises from the dead." (Luke 16:29-31)

They didn't know it yet, but someone was about to rise from the dead. Jesus was going to rise from the dead and offer that resurrection to us.

When I was in college, I was the "Come on, let's . . ." guy. I think it's how I compensated for everyone thinking I was still in high school (I was a late bloomer.). My goal in college was to get as many people to do something as possible, and it was awesome. I'd say, "Hey, let's go get a Coke," "Hey, let's go to Taco Bell," "Hey, let's go out for ice cream!" Yes, I grew three inches in college in both directions. Then we graduated, and people started getting married and having kids. But Darci and I were late bloomers there too. All our friends were having kids, and we were still in college mode. We wanted to go to a movie, but they wanted to put their kids to bed at 8 p.m.

Let's go back to gathering crowds, to doing life together, to inviting strangers, and to building relationships outside our immediate families. Let's reach out to lonely and hurting people. Let's open our doors.

Reflect: Who has God placed in your life that needs the kind of love our selfish world often withholds?

35

Childlike Humility

Accompanying Scripture Reading: Matthew 19:13–26

FOR MOST OF HUMAN history, the firstborn son has received the birthright from his family. Kings gave their crowns and fathers gave control of their homes to their firstborn sons, but God consistently breaks the rules of this cultural norm. God regularly elevated the second-born son. He elevated Abel over Cain, Isaac over Ishmael, and Jacob over Esau.

> The Son is the image of the invisible God, the firstborn over all creation. (Col 1:15 NIV)

The apostle Paul describes Jesus as a firstborn, but what did Jesus do with the power he received as the firstborn? He gave it up. Jesus was a king, but he did not wield physical power:

CHILDLIKE HUMILITY

> Instead, he gave up his divine privileges; he took the humble position of a slave and was born as a human being. (Phil 2:7)

Jesus is the king of an upside-down kingdom that puts others before self:

> But Jesus called them together and said, "You know that the rulers in this world lord it over their people, and officials flaunt their authority over those under them. But among you it will be different. Whoever wants to be a leader among you must be your servant." (Matt 20:25-26)

When Jesus lived on earth, 50 percent of the children died before adulthood.[1] So, kids didn't have much value until they had proven that they were superior to the rest. For most of human history, people had to fight for status. Respect and honor were not simply given, but Jesus changed all of that. Jesus taught us that everyone has value because everyone is created in God's image.

One day, Jesus had just finished healing many sick people when some parents brought their children to Jesus. These parents recognized Jesus' power and hoped that power could protect their children. If people believe Jesus has something to offer their kids, they will bring their kids to Jesus. In that way, Jesus is irresistible. The strange thing about this story is not that people brought their kids to Jesus, but that Jesus accepted them. Jesus' disciples attempted to keep the children away, but Jesus invited them to come closer:

> But Jesus said, "Let the children come to me. Don't stop them! For the Kingdom of Heaven belongs to those who are like these children." (Matt 19:14)

The world assumed Jesus wouldn't have time for people with as little value as children. Jesus could have spent all of his time with religious and political leaders, but Jesus gave his time to widows and orphans. In fact, Jesus prioritized young people. Why? Because cynicism hadn't had the time to overtake them to the point where they wouldn't hear what he had to say. In other words, ministry to kids is more effective, more fruitful.

Not long before Jesus invited these children to come to him, he used children as an example, an illustration of the kind of attitude we should all have:

1. "Child Mortality."

> Jesus called a little child to him and put the child among them. Then he said, "I tell you the truth, unless you turn from your sins and become like little children, you will never get into the Kingdom of Heaven. So anyone who becomes as humble as this little child is the greatest in the Kingdom of Heaven." (Matt 18:2–4)

This is the passage the church has traditionally used to emphasize the importance of "childlike faith," but that phrase does not show up in the Bible. This passage is about childlike humility. Jesus was answering a question about who is greatest, and he pointed to the humblest of the people around him.

Sometimes, the strength, success, experience, and knowledge we accumulate causes us to become prideful. For our faith to mature, we have to put all of that behind us and recognize that we are totally dependent on God. The distance between God's goodness and my goodness is almost identical to the distance between God's goodness and the worst sinner's goodness. Why is that? Because God is that great. Compared to God's goodness, we are all bad.

This week, with honest sincerity, my son asked me if there is anyone in the world who is stronger than I am. I lied and said, "No." Because there is such a great difference between his strength and my strength, he assumes I am strong. But compared to the average oil-field worker in my church, I am weak.

The Beethoven-Haus is a museum in Bonn, Germany, for the great composer and pianist Ludwig van Beethoven. One of Beethoven's pianos is on display in that museum, and the museum guards work to keep the piano in top condition. They are tasked with protecting the piano because when children see the piano, they attempt to play it. However, when the great pianists of our time visit the location to reflect on the greatness of Ludwig van Beethoven, they never attempt to play the piano. The adults admire the man rather than play with the man. What a waste. Pianos were meant to be played, not simply looked at.

When we work hard to build a beautiful and moral life, we are tempted to admire our efforts and proudly display our goodness. Any growth we have experienced should only be used to point people to Jesus. Our good works serve as tools to glorify God, not to glorify ourselves. If we truly see the goodness of God, we cannot be proud. When we truly know ourselves, we will be humbled.

Childlike Humility

Can I be content when no one compliments me yet glorifies God? Am I tempted to believe I have arrived at a summit when I have only reached the base camp? Childlike humility leads us to worship and to prayer. It causes us to surrender to God's will rather than to invite God into our will.

Reflect: What is the difference between demonstrating your own goodness and reflecting God's goodness?

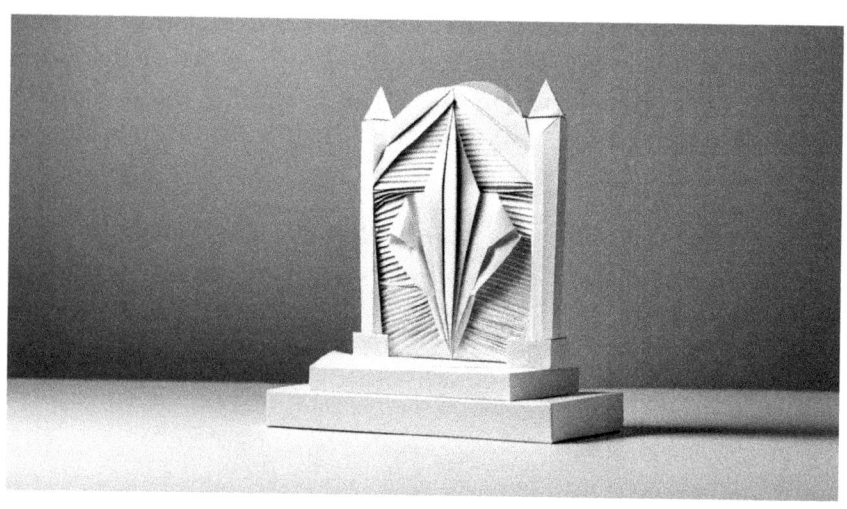

36

Waiting on Jesus

Accompanying Scripture Reading: John 11:1–44

BECAUSE GOD IS AN eternal being who lives outside of time and space, we cannot believe in God without believing he is capable of supernatural activity. It is tempting to explain away the stories found in the Bible by pointing to potential scientific explanations of supernatural events, but the key events of human history cannot be explained with scientifically verifiable phenomenon.

The eternal narrative of Scripture may seem unrealistic, but so do a lot of the supernatural acts of God. Enlightenment rationality is valuable, but its value is limited. It cannot give us access to the truth we need for a meaningful life. Biblical truth is not comfortable in the modern materialistic narrative because the Bible is full of unexplainable events. Scripture is too comprehensive to fit neatly into the power schemes and scientific theories of the world. It doesn't fit into the world's narrative because biblical truth is the only true metanarrative. If it's not, it is simply a lie. Because the Bible claims to be the word of the eternal God, it cannot simply be a book of wisdom or history lessons.

The eleventh chapter of Luke contains a story about the most surprising and unexplainable form of miracle, a resurrection. A resurrection creates life where there was only death. Science is completely incapable of creating conscious life, but that's God's signature move. Only God can create life from non-life. He has done it throughout history, and he can do it in your life.

Have you ever felt completely hopeless? Have you ever felt like God was forcing you to wait for something? What do you do when your questions go unanswered, when you feel God could intervene but doesn't? What do you do when God doesn't do what you think he should? Is it really true that God offers hope for hurting people? Is there purpose in our pain?

If we were honest, we would all admit that there has been a time or two in our lives when we question if the One who is running this universe is asleep at the wheel. In these times, we say to God, "Where were you when I needed you?"

Let me tell you about a family in the Bible who had to wrestle with these same emotions. They felt that Jesus had failed to help when he could have. These were close friends of Jesus, and he seems to have been a frequent guest at their home. This family consisted of at least three siblings: Mary, Martha, and Lazarus.

Lazarus, who lived in Bethany, became very sick. Unfortunately, Jesus and his disciples were nowhere near Bethany at the time. So, Jesus got a frantic message from Lazarus's sisters asking him to return to help their brother. They were calling in a favor to their good friend Jesus. They were probably thinking, "Jesus, you're always healing strangers; now your best friend is dying. Come help!"

The story is found in John 11:

> But when Jesus heard about it he said, "Lazarus's sickness will not end in death. No, it happened for the glory of God so that the Son of God will receive glory from this." So although Jesus loved Martha, Mary, and Lazarus, he stayed where he was for the next two days. (John 11:4–6)

There are two unique statements in that passage: one made by Jesus and one by John. Jesus chose his words carefully when he said, "This sickness won't end in death." Jesus was inviting his followers to trust him. Then,

John pointed out something he wanted the reader to remember throughout the story. He told us that Jesus loved Mary, Martha, and Lazarus.

When Jesus heard the message about his good friend's illness, you would think that he would have immediately grabbed his backpack and run to Bethany shouting, "My guy needs me!" But that's not what happened. Instead, he took his time.

What is going on here? Why is Jesus pausing? Let's divide the story into four phases. The first phase is "waiting."

1. Waiting

When Jesus and the disciples finally start walking to Bethany, the sisters are very angry. They're waiting, but Jesus isn't coming. By the time Jesus arrives in Bethany, Lazarus has been dead for four days.

How do you respond when God makes you wait? Maybe you've been trying to buy a house, but the market has skyrocketed. So, you wait. Maybe you've wanted grandchildren, but your adult children seem more interested in climbing the ladder at work than making you a grandma. Maybe you keep waiting for a promotion at work, but your boss keeps putting off his retirement. So, you wait.

Waiting can be very discouraging! Even though we spend so much of our lives waiting, most of us aren't particularly good at it, and we would definitely never choose it. No one walks into a store, gets their stuff, then sizes up the cashiers to pick the slowest line.

In our minds, "wait" means "late" and late is never a good thing. So, we ask God to intervene: "Lord, please hurry." We say, "Fix our marriage, heal my sickness, help me make the team, transfer my boss!" But God might be up to something, and while you're waiting, he's working. A waiting season is never a wasted season. Sometimes God wants to do something in you before he does something through you.

Waiting is even harder when we don't have all the information. Sometimes we don't even know what we are waiting for. So, the second phase of the story is "wondering."

2. Wondering

Jesus explained to his disciples that Lazarus was sleeping, but they didn't understand:

Waiting on Jesus

> So he told them plainly, "Lazarus is dead. And for your sakes, I'm glad I wasn't there, for now you will really believe. Come, let's go see him." (John 11:14–15)

Jesus was preparing for what would happen a few days later, but the disciples had no idea what was going to unfold. This is foreshadowing. Jesus waited so they would believe.

At this point, there are more questions than answers. In some situations, that's how it will be until we are in heaven, but eventually we will understand. Eventually, our eyes will be opened to the full reality of our lives, and all of the pain and frustration will make more sense. Maybe you're in a season where the pain is so potent that you're just trying to survive. Here's the good news: God is on the throne. He has a plan.

Before heaven, there's a lot of the third phase of the story, which is "hurting."

3. Hurting

Christ's waiting hurt Lazarus's sisters, Mary and Martha. His failure to drop what he was doing and return immediately was too painful for them to swallow. So they ran out to Jesus to express their displeasure:

> Lord, if only you had been here, my brother would not have died. (John 11:21)

They were angry. They were in pain because they thought that Jesus was too late. This brings us to the fourth phase of the story. After Jesus wept with the sisters, he asked them to take him to Lazarus' grave and instructed them to roll away the stone that covered the tomb.

We will read the next part of the story in the King James translation because it's much more entertaining:

> Martha, the sister of him that was dead, saith unto him, "Lord, by this time he stinketh: for he hath been dead four days." (John 11:39 KJV)

Jesus waited four days to prove that Lazarus was dead. When they rolled away the stone, there was no one left wondering if Lazarus was dead. If there had been any doubters, the stink would have convinced them. That's when Jesus chose to resurrect Lazarus:

> Then Jesus shouted, "Lazarus, come out!" And the dead man came out, his hands and feet bound in graveclothes, his face wrapped in

a headcloth. Jesus told them, "Unwrap him and let him go!" (Luke 11:43–44)

Everyone was "waiting." The disciples were "wondering." The sisters were "hurting." But God was "working."

4. Working

Jesus wanted the people to realize he was the Messiah. The delay was motivated by love. Jesus loves us, and that is why he demonstrates his deity to us. He wants us to know he is the Messiah, because knowing him is greater than physical health:

> The Lord isn't really being slow about his promise, as some people think. No, he is being patient for your sake. He does not want anyone to be destroyed, but wants everyone to repent. (2 Pet 3:9)

We can trust God's timing:

> So let's not get tired of doing what is good. At just the right time we will reap a harvest of blessing if we don't give up. (Gal 6:9)

Our harvest might come in this life or the next. Either way, a physical death is not the worst thing that can happen to us. The worst thing that can happen to us is to die without a relationship with Jesus Christ. Sometimes, because God knows everything, his answer to our request might be "no," but don't get tired of doing what is good. Don't give up, because at just the right time, we will reap a harvest of blessing.

Reflect: Talk to God about something you recently asked him for and ask him to help you see his plan and understand his timing.

37

Be Righteous

Accompanying Scripture Reading: Luke 19:1–10

HAVE YOU EVER MET a famous person who you really admired? Maybe you got starstruck and said something dumb. Have you ever wondered what would happen if that person showed up at your house?

There's a story in the Bible about a guy named Zacchaeus who wanted to see Jesus. By this time in Jesus' life, he was famous. He was constantly surrounded by crowds, and Zacchaeus wanted to see him. Unfortunately, Zacchaeus couldn't see Jesus for two reasons. First, he was a sinner. Zacchaeus was a tax collector. To the Hebrew people, tax collectors were seen as the worst kind of sinner. How could a tax collector get close to a religious leader like Jesus? The second reason Zacchaeus couldn't see Jesus was his height. Zacchaeus was noticeably short, and Jesus' disciples didn't have any cameras or giant LED screens handy. That's why Zacchaeus decided to climb a tree:

> So he ran ahead and climbed a sycamore-fig tree beside the road, for Jesus was going to pass that way. When Jesus came by, he looked up at Zacchaeus and called him by name. "Zacchaeus!" he said. "Quick, come down! I must be a guest in your home today." Zacchaeus quickly climbed down and took Jesus to his house in great excitement and joy. But the people were displeased. "He has gone to be the guest of a notorious sinner," they grumbled. (Luke 19:4–7)

This sinner shouldn't even be allowed near Jesus, yet Jesus went to his house! Zacchaeus recognized the amazing power and value in what Jesus was teaching. It seems that everyone else was just there because it was the most interesting place to be. Jesus was surrounded by people who were jumping on the religious bandwagon, but Zacchaeus recognized that there was more to what Jesus was teaching than just religious talk.

That's why people got mad at Jesus. They didn't understand that Jesus had come to turn the religious system on its head. Jesus recognized Zacchaeus's faith and that Zacchaeus had actually heard his teaching and believed. Because Zacchaeus believed, God counted him as righteous. The religious system of Jesus' day ascribed righteousness to people who behaved, but Jesus ascribed righteousness to people who believed:

> For the Scriptures tell us, "Abraham believed God, and God counted him as righteous because of his faith." (Rom 4:3)

To this day, our sinful nature attempts to earn righteousness, but that is an impossible task. We judge people by comparing them to our own goodness, but that's not how judges are meant to make judgments. Judges compare actions to the law, not to their own behavior. When a standard or a law is created, all actions that fail to meet that standard are judged as indictable. The standard that we are commanded to meet is perfection. We are commanded to be like Jesus, and Jesus is perfect:

> You are to be perfect, even as your Father in heaven is perfect. (Matt 5:48)

Jesus didn't go to Zacchaeus's house because Zacchaeus was righteous. Jesus went to Zacchaeus's house because Jesus was righteous, and Jesus' righteousness was given to Zacchaeus when Zacchaeus put his faith in Jesus.

Does Christ's gift of righteousness mean good behavior is unnecessary or meaningless? No. In fact, when Jesus gives his righteousness to us, the Holy Spirit comes with that righteousness. His kindness is meant to lead us to repentance. The gift of God's grace cleanses us of unrighteousness and makes us worthy to become the temple of the Holy Spirit. When this happens, God's spirit lives in us and changes us. If we are not being changed, if we are not growing in faith and spiritual maturity, God's spirit does not live in us.

A relationship with Jesus will change us like it changed Zacchaeus. When Zacchaeus put his faith in Jesus, Zacchaeus was radically and rapidly changed:

> Meanwhile, Zacchaeus stood before the Lord and said, "I will give half my wealth to the poor, Lord, and if I have cheated people on their taxes, I will give them back four times as much!" Jesus responded, "Salvation has come to this home today, for this man has shown himself to be a true son of Abraham. For the Son of Man came to seek and save those who are lost." (Luke 19:8–10)

Zacchaeus was a true son of Abraham because he had faith like Abraham, and that faith brought salvation to Zacchaeus. Before he had a relationship with Jesus, Zacchaeus was lost. When he believed the old religious lies that his sinful behavior disqualified him from a relationship with God, Zacchaeus was a slave to his sinful desires. When Jesus came to his home, Jesus brought sanctifying righteousness with him.

Never expect someone to clean up their life before they begin a relationship with God. That kind of judgment will only lead people to legalism and self-righteousness.

Recently, protestors who call themselves Christians, but act like Pharisees, have shown up on Sunday mornings outside our church with signs and megaphones to condemn our members. They say we allow too many sinners to attend our services. They say we should add more sins to our list and a hierarchy of publicly condemned sins.

Instead, our strategy is to schedule encounters between Jesus and sinful people because we believe that a relationship with Jesus changes everything, every time:

> It is the same with my word. I send it out, and it always produces fruit. It will accomplish all I want it to, and it will prosper everywhere I send it. (Isa 55:11)

God might not change people on our timeline or according to our priorities, but salvation is assured. He saves us from eternal punishment, and he saves us from the bondage that our sin creates. He who calls you is faithful. Jesus came to seek and save those who are lost, not to congratulate the self-righteous.

Reflect: When you're tempted to judge people for not living like Christ before or soon after they follow him, how can you shift your perspective to see them through Christ's grace-filled eyes?

38

Donkeys Beat Horses

Accompanying Scripture Reading: Matthew 21:1–11

THE PASSION WEEK, THE final week of Jesus' earthly ministry, culminates in his crucifixion and resurrection. It began with Jesus' triumphal entry into Jerusalem, a significant event during the Jewish festival of Passover when pilgrims gathered in Jerusalem. Just days before this entry, Jesus had raised Lazarus from the dead in Bethany, causing a stir among the people and leading many to believe in him (John 12:17–18). As Jesus approached Jerusalem, he sent two disciples ahead to fetch a donkey. This act, where Jesus entered the city amidst shouts of praise and waving palm branches, was a public declaration of his kingship and messianic identity.

As Jesus and his disciples approached Jerusalem, they came to the village of Bethphage on the Mount of Olives. Jesus sent two disciples ahead with instructions to bring him a donkey and its colt, saying, "The Lord needs them." The disciples did as Jesus instructed, bringing the donkey and colt, and placing their cloaks on them. A large crowd gathered, spreading their cloaks and palm branches on the road, and shouting praises (Matt 21:9).

The choice of a donkey over a horse is deeply symbolic. In ancient times, a horse was often associated with war and military conquest,[1] while here a donkey symbolizes peace and humility. By entering Jerusalem on a donkey, Jesus deliberately fulfilled the prophecy of Zech 9:9:

> Rejoice, O people of Zion!
> Shout in triumph, O people of Jerusalem!
> Look, your king is coming to you.
> He is righteous and victorious,
> yet he is humble, riding on a donkey—
> riding on a donkey's colt. (Zech 9:9)

> Look, your King is coming to you. He is humble, riding on a donkey—riding on a donkey's colt. (Matt 21:5)

This humble mode of transport was a stark contrast to the typical grand entrances of earthly kings who would ride majestic horses, showcasing their power and authority. Jesus' choice of a donkey emphasized his mission of peace and reconciliation rather than domination and conflict. How does this picture of Jesus compute with your understanding of who Jesus is?

When you ask Jesus for things, do you expect his power to be used to make your life easier or more luxurious? Do you expect that following Jesus will make you wealthier? In some ways it does. The proverbs and teachings found in the Bible cause us to live frugally and responsibly, and those actions do lead to more healthy financial situations. The wisdom of Scripture will make us more successful. It can lead to promotions at work, financial blessings, and investment success. Jesus will make our lives better, but he will also lead us to sacrificial generosity and to humility. The blessed life will be a life that brings glory to God, not to us.

The crowd's reaction to Jesus' entry was one of excitement and praise. They spread their cloaks and palm branches on the road, a traditional way to honor someone of great importance. This act of laying down cloaks and waving palm branches demonstrates several key things. By laying their cloaks on the road, the people showed great reverence and humility before Jesus. This was an act of submission, acknowledging Jesus' authority and kingship. In ancient times, cloaks were valuable possessions—as evidenced by the Roman soldiers gambling for Jesus' clothes after crucifying

---

1. Tallis, "Horses and Human History."

him (Matt 27:35–37)—and laying them down was a significant gesture of respect and honor. The palm branches symbolized victory and triumph.[2] By waving them, the crowd expressed their recognition of Jesus' role and their willingness to serve and worship him. This act signifies their readiness to support Jesus and align with his mission. Their shouts of "Praise God for the Son of David! Blessings on the one who comes in the name of the Lord!" reflect their hope for deliverance. The term "Hosanna" means "save now," showing the crowd's desire for salvation and a better future.

The triumphal entry of Jesus challenges our modern views of leadership. In today's world, leadership is often associated with charisma, authority, and assertiveness. Many leadership theories emphasize strategic decision-making, influence tactics, and organizational effectiveness. However, the example of Jesus riding on a donkey offers a profound contrast. His leadership was characterized by humility, service, and a focus on relational rather than transactional outcomes. Jesus did not rely on instinctual leadership prowess or follow contemporary leadership science. Instead, he embodied God's plan for leadership—a plan centered on sacrificial love and genuine care for others.

Jesus could have had the best of everything. He could have eaten the best food, stayed in the finest hotels, and had unlimited servants. Instead, he lived amongst the outcasts of his world. He could have had a servant who washed his feet, but he washed the feet of his disciples (John 13:5).

Jesus' approach to leadership challenges us to reconsider what it means to lead effectively. Rather than seeking short-term activity or immediate compliance, Jesus aimed for lasting impact and transformation of hearts. His ministry was about winning over hearts through love and compassion, not forcing obedience through fear or authority. This model of leadership encourages us to prioritize relationships and the well-being of others above personal gain or status. It invites us to bow down to God's plan for leadership, trusting in his wisdom and guidance rather than relying solely on human strategies.

In our roles as leaders, whether in our families, workplaces, or communities, we can learn from Jesus' example. Christlike leadership involves genuine humility, a willingness to serve, and a commitment to fostering peace and unity. It requires us to listen attentively, understand deeply, and act compassionately. What does Christlike leadership look like in your context? How can you emulate Jesus' humility and service in your daily interactions?

2. Jacobs, "Meaning of Palm Branches."

As we reflect on Jesus' triumphal entry, we are invited to embrace his model of leadership. Let us strive to lead in a way that reflects the heart of Jesus, bringing hope, healing, and transformation to those around us. May our lives, like Jesus' entry into Jerusalem, proclaim the coming of God's kingdom—a kingdom of peace, justice, and abundant life for all.

Reflect: When you lead, is it more difficult to prioritize the well-being of others, to seek reconciliation over division, or to value relationships over authority?

39

Throw Tables

Accompanying Scripture Reading: Matthew 21:12–17

ON OCTOBER 16, 1981, before I was born, my family was driving on K-15, a two-lane highway between Derby, Kansas, and Mulvane, Kansas. They were driving a 1972 Ford station wagon with paneling. For those of you who were born after 1985, that's stick-on wood. They packed ten people into the car for my oldest sister, Jeanna's, birthday party. Dad was driving. My oldest brother, Bill, was in the front bench seat with Mom and Dad. My other sister, Rebekah, was in the middle seat with her friends, and Jeanna was in the back seat (the seat that faced backward) with her friends. None of them were wearing seat belts. They didn't even consider wearing seat belts. Suddenly, a drunk driver came barreling toward them in their lane and hit them head-on at full speed. There was blood everywhere. A few of them lost all their teeth. My brother ended up with an engine in his lap.

Dad passed out trying to get Mom out of the car. One of the girls who was just there for the birthday party had a concussion and began walking down the street, having no idea what she was doing or where she was. It wasn't the birthday party Jeanna expected.

Why didn't my family wear seat belts? Because cultural norms dictate behavior. Car manufacturers started putting seat belts in cars in the 1960s, but nobody wore them back then. Today, because of cultural norms, most people drive five miles per hour over the speed limit even though it is literally called a "limit." Cultural norms can override limits.

If cultural norms are such a powerful force, what does it take to change a cultural norm? The answer is "catastrophe." Catastrophe changes culture because catastrophes lead some people to pursue change.

A few years after my family's catastrophic car accident, I was born. The first car I can remember us owning was a 1984 burgundy Mercury Grand Marquis. You would assume after experiencing such a terrible wreck my family would ensure that I always sat in the back seat, strapped down with a seat belt, but that's not what happened. Because we had a large family, I often laid on the back window ledge or sat on the armrest in the front seat. I guess you could say I was the hump boy. If dad slammed on the brakes too hard, I would have been a projectile missile, flying through the window into oncoming traffic.

So, I guess the real question is, "Why didn't my parents love me?"

What finally changed my parents' behavior? A law and a campaign, "Click It or Ticket." At first, the use of seat belts was a suggestion ("people are dying!"), but most people ignored the suggestion. In the meantime, a few people began campaigning for laws that would force people to change their behavior.

Now, cars beep at you until you put your seat belt on. If you don't, I think it sends an electric shock up your spine. We force parents to harness their infants in a car seat tight enough to cut off the circulation in their legs. Fairly quickly the world went from completely unaware that seat belts were necessary to a culture that judges people who don't wear seat belts.

This happens to people spiritually all the time. They might be living in joyous ignorance of the dangers of life and the consequence of sin until something happens to make them aware of the fact that the punishment for sin is eternal death. This often happens when people hear truth preached, and they recognize there is a God. Tragedy and pain also make people aware that changes need to be made. Sometimes people make many bad decisions, and when they hit rock bottom, they turn to God. When we are living in ignorance, we need a wake-up call.

Jonathan Edwards is one of history's most famous preachers. Edwards preached ten times as many sermons about heaven than about hell, but when he preached the famous sermon "Sinners in the Hands of an Angry God," everyone listened.[1] The sermon became famous because it was a wake-up call.

After Christ's triumphal entry, he went to the temple. As Jesus arrived at the temple, he encountered a scene of commerce overwhelming the sacred space. People traded animals for sacrifices and money changers busily conducted transactions. Enraged, Jesus overturned the tables:

> [Jesus] said to them, "The Scriptures declare, 'My Temple will be called a house of prayer,' but you have turned it into a den of thieves!" (Matt 21:13)

This story from the life of Jesus is unlike any of the other stories that we know of from his life. Jesus never acted like this. So, what motivated Jesus to act this way? Let's ask a few questions of this story:

1. Why did Jesus kick over the tables?

One of the reasons Jesus turned over the tables was to fight against greed. When God made the Jewish sacrificial system, he required Jews to sacrifice animals at the temple, and people were forced to travel long distances to make these sacrifices. For that reason, entrepreneurs realized an opportunity to make some money. They sold animals to pilgrimaging Jews so people wouldn't have to travel across the country with their animals. Unfortunately, they did this for personal gain, not to help people act in obedience to the law. Rather than helping these pilgrims, they were price gouging even though God wrote into the old covenant some allowances for poor people to sacrifice less expensive animals. The Jews should have helped people get animals, not use God's law to take advantage of people.

When Jesus called the temple a den of thieves, he was quoting Jer 7:11:

> Don't you yourselves admit that this Temple, which bears my name, has become a den of thieves?

This passage makes it more obvious why the religious leaders hated Jesus. When Jeremiah said this, he was warning Israel that the temple was

---

1. Edwards, "Sinners in the Hands."

going to be destroyed, and Jesus was prophesying the same thing. The temple was again going to be destroyed.

Jesus was also angry at the temple that day because he witnessed sinful discrimination.

Many Christians use this story to justify arbitrary laws about selling things in a church building, but that is not the point of this story at all. Jesus was in the temple, but he was not in the sanctuary. He was in the outer courtyard. In Herod's Temple, the outer courtyard was reserved for gentiles to worship God. In other words, the Jews were taking the gentile's worshiping space from them. When Jesus said the temple was to be a house of prayer, he was quoting Isaiah:

> I will bring them to my holy mountain of Jerusalem and will fill them with joy in my house of prayer. I will accept their burnt offerings and sacrifices, because my Temple will be called a house of prayer for all nations. (Isa 56:7)

The temple on Mount Moriah was meant to be a house of prayer for all nations, not only the Jews, but the Jews were crowding out the other nations.

The second question that must be asked of this story is about anger:

2. Is anger a sin?

This story is one of only two or three stories in the Bible in which Jesus got mad. In each story, Jesus was angry at religious leaders. Jesus never sinned, but he did get angry. When Jesus gets angry, it is righteous anger.

Unlike Jesus, we are sinners. We can't trust our anger because our emotions often cloud our minds. Too often, anger breaks relationships. When you are angry, ask yourself, "Is this worth breaking a relationship?" Run from anger. If CNN makes you mad, stop watching it. If you get angry when you drink alcohol, stop drinking.

When my sons get angry, I tell them to take deep breaths. It makes them slow down. When we slow down, we have time to make a choice. Renew your mind. Pray. Breathe.

> In your anger do not sin: Do not let the sun go down while you are still angry. (Eph 4:26)

Anger usually happens when someone takes something from us or hurts us. Anger usually involves a statement like, "I deserve," "That's not fair," or "It's my right." The root of sinful anger is selfishness. Spiritual maturity reduces anger because it removes the focus from self to God. As we mature spiritually, we set our eyes on things above.

God gets angry when people get in the way of other people worshiping. When my preference of how we worship, or who we worship with, gets in the way of people worshiping God, I'm sinning.

If you know a certain situation tends to make you angry, pray before you go there. Set your mind on things above. Think about the big picture. Before you go into a situation that could anger you, think about the relationships that might be hurt if you lose control of your anger.

> We demolish arguments and every pretension that sets itself up against the knowledge of God, and we take captive every thought to make it obedient to Christ. (2 Cor 10:5)

Take your angry thoughts captive. Lay anger on the altar and sacrifice it to God.

Reflect: What generally makes you angry, and how can you make a plan to avoid sinful anger?

40

Christians Love

Accompanying Scripture Reading: Matthew 22:34–40

AT THE HEART OF Christian teaching lies the Great Commandment, a profound principle that captures the essence of our faith. When Jesus was asked about the greatest commandment, his response was both simple and profound, anchoring everything in love:

> Jesus replied, "'You must love the Lord your God with all your heart, all your soul, and all your mind.' This is the first and greatest commandment. A second is equally important: 'Love your neighbor as yourself.' The entire law and all the demands of the prophets are based on these two commandments." (Matt 22:37–40)

Most of the greatest lovers in human history have been Christians. Their motivation to love God led them to love people in extravagantly selfless ways. Without Christian love, the world would not be completely devoid of love because the prevenient grace of God and the imprint of his image on our hearts lead us to love, but without Christian love, our world would be a much more divided, selfish, and angry place. Loving God with everything we have is directly connected to loving our neighbors as ourselves. These aren't two separate commands, but two parts of the same whole. They're inseparable, reflecting the full nature of love as God intends.

It's important to realize that the love Jesus commands goes beyond feelings. Today, we often think of love as an emotion, something we feel deeply, but biblical love, especially the kind Jesus talks about, is active and intentional. It's about actions and choices, not only feelings.

Jesus gives a powerful example of this active love in John 13:14–15 when he washes his disciples' feet and then tells them to follow his example, to wash each others' feet. This act of service and humility shows love as an action.

If you love me, obey my commandments. (John 14:15)

The love Jesus commands shows itself in obedience and service, reflecting our commitment to God through how we treat others.

When Jesus gave the Great Commandment, he was responding to a question the Pharisees asked him about which of Moses' commandments was most important. Jesus' answer to the Pharisees is brilliant in its simplicity and depth. By summarizing the law and the prophets with these two commandments, Jesus captures the entirety of Old Testament teaching. The many laws given to the Israelites were meant to guide them in living a life of love toward God and others. Jesus distills these complex laws into a call for relational love—love that is both vertical (toward God) and horizontal (toward people).

To love God with all our being means committing every aspect of our lives to him. It means prioritizing our relationship with him above all else, allowing his love to transform us from within. This transformation naturally flows outward in the form of loving others. When we truly love God, we begin to see others through his eyes, leading us to act with compassion, kindness, and generosity.

C. S. Lewis famously talked about the four types of love in the Greek New Testament: *storge* (family love), *philia* (friendship), *eros* (romantic love), and *agape* (unconditional love).[1] Agape love, the most mature and selfless form, is what Jesus most uniquely embodies and commands. This

---

1. Lewis, *Four Loves*.

love isn't contingent on the worthiness of its recipient, but is given freely and unconditionally.

Agape love is generous. It seeks the good of others without expecting anything in return. It mirrors the love God has for us, a love that gave his only Son for our redemption. This generous love is the hallmark of true Christian living. It's the love that Jesus modeled throughout his ministry and, ultimately, on the cross.

> If someone says, "I love God," but hates a fellow believer, that person is a liar; for if we don't love people we can see, how can we love God, whom we cannot see? (1 John 4:20)

Genuine love for God will inevitably result in love for others. Our interactions with people become the proving ground of our professed love for God. When we engage in acts of kindness, forgiveness, and service, we're not just loving those around us; we're honoring God. Each act of love towards others reflects our devotion to God. It's through these actions that the world sees the reality of God's love manifested in us.

> Truly I tell you, whatever you did for one of the least of these brothers and sisters of mine, you did for me. (Matt 25:40)

If we could perfectly obey the Great Commandment, we'd naturally fulfill all other commands that are beneficial for a healthy and united life. Our love for God would be reflected in our love for others, encompassing every moral directive given by God.

There are some laws in the old covenant that God made with Israel that do not have a direct correlation with loving others. In the old covenant, established between God and Israel, there are numerous laws that go beyond the straightforward principle of loving others. These laws encompass a wide array of directives, including ceremonial, dietary, and ritualistic regulations that were specific to the cultural and religious context of ancient Israel. For instance, laws concerning animal sacrifices, the observance of specific festivals, and restrictions on certain foods were primarily designed to set Israel apart as a holy nation and to guide their worship practices. While these laws served important functions within their covenant relationship with God, they do not directly correlate with the ethical command to love others. Instead, they focus on maintaining purity, religious identity, and obedience to God's covenantal requirements, but it can easily be argued that it was in the best interest of the Jewish people to live this countercultural lifestyle. By living differently than the nations around them, they separated themselves from the tempting secular customs of those cultures. By obeying those commands, they loved their neighbors by leading them away from the pagan practices of the world and toward the holy traditions of the Jewish people.

The Great Commandment calls us to a life of active, generous love. It reminds us that our relationship with God is deeply interconnected with our relationship with others. We can't claim to love God while neglecting to love those made in his image. In loving others, we fulfill the law and the prophets, and we demonstrate the transformative power of God's love in our lives. Let's strive to embody God's love daily, knowing that in doing so, we are fulfilling the greatest commandment given by our Lord. This is the essence of our faith and the path to true Christian maturity.

Reflect: Do you find it more difficult to demonstrate love for God or for people?

41

Afraid of Antichrists

Accompanying Scripture Reading: Matthew 24:4–44

I GREW UP TERRIFIED of the antichrist. My family went to a dispensational church where we were taught that there is an evil antichrist coming who will control the world and kill all the Christians he can, and he will cut off your head if you say you're a Christian. However, if you deny Christ so that you don't get your head cut off, you go to hell. It felt like a no-win situation. We were terrified of the antichrist, and because we were so scared of him, we found him everywhere. We thought every president with whom we disagreed was the antichrist. Every famous musician and every military leader we didn't like was the antichrist... until we realized they weren't.

What does all this fear lead to? Bunkering. It tempts us to separate ourselves from the world and hide our comfortable lives from the terrifying world. If this is what our theology leads us to, and it is a true theology, we should learn how to live on mission in a dangerous world without separating from it. But I do not believe that interpretation of Scripture is accurate.

In Matt 24, Jesus prophesies terrifying events that can easily incite fear: the abomination of desolation and a great tribulation. This passage does come with a warning about these terrifying events that directs readers to run and hide when these events happen. Some Christians believe these events will happen in the future, and every generation that believed that, also believed those events would happen in their lifetime. I believe that the abomination of desolation and the great tribulation that Jesus talked about have already happened. They happened in the first century when the Roman army destroyed the temple. The events of the first century fulfill every detail of Jesus' prophecy, but the focus of Jesus' statements was on the endurance of God's family.

The one who endures to the end will be saved. (Matt 24:13)

When we talk about the antichrist, three New Testament passages usually come up: 2 Thess 2 (the man of lawlessness), 1 John 2 (the antichrist), and Rev 13 (the beast). We have a habit of assuming these three people are the same person, but the Bible doesn't say they are. Let's go quickly through each, starting with the last one.

Revelation 13 introduces the idea of kingdoms referred to as beasts. When it comes to the beast in Revelation, no one fulfilled the beast prophecies more than Rome and Emperor Nero. Nero mocked God's creation,[1] killed his mom,[2] kicked his wife in the stomach killing her and her unborn baby,[3] and dressed a male slave up like his wife then married him.[4] He crucified Peter upside down[5] and beheaded Paul. Rome destroyed the Jerusalem temple.[6] When you add up the Hebrew numbers in the name Nero, you get 666.[7]

But that doesn't mean there haven't been more beasts since Nero. We've witnessed the evils of Diocletian, Stalin, and Pol Pot. The good news is all these beasts were defeated. Don't fear them. In fact, the persecution of the beasts has always sparked Christian church growth.

1. Hulme, "Messiahs!"
2. Hansley, "Emperor Nero."
3. Lewis, "Poppaea Sabina."
4. Carmean, "Sporus and Nero."
5. Oakes, "What Is the Evidence."
6. Lohnes, "Siege of Jerusalem."
7. Malik, "Nero Versus the Christians."

The passage in Rev 13 is also the passage that predicts the mark of the beast. Many believe that the mark of the beast will be a forced tattoo or microchip, but I find that hard to believe. Revelation also tells us we are to get God's mark on our forehead. We get this vision of Jesus' return in Rev 9:4:

> They were told not to harm the grass or plants or trees, but only the people who did not have the seal of God on their foreheads.

Does this passage instruct us to get 777 tattooed on our forehead or to insert a microchip under our skin? No. Being marked is swearing allegiance. It's choosing to follow. The instruction of Rev 13 is to choose not to follow the beast.

Now let's look at the second passage. In 1 John 2, John said there will be many antichrists, not just one. They are what Jesus called wolves in sheep's clothing. Unlike the beasts, they claim to be one of us. However, in the last hour, they will harm the Christian mission. So, when is the last hour?

> The last hour is here. You have heard that the Antichrist is coming, and already many such antichrists have appeared. (1 John 2:18)

John did not say the last hour is coming someday. He's prophesying events that are already beginning to happen in his lifetime. He then talks about the antichrists' presence in his world.

When he says antichrists have already come, Paul is talking about people like Caligula. Caligula was a Roman emperor who tried to put a statue of himself in the Jerusalem temple to be worshiped. This passage claims that antichrists will try to lead Christians astray by claiming that Jesus is not God, but we shouldn't be deceived by their lies:

> And who is a liar? Anyone who says that Jesus is not the Christ. Anyone who denies the Father and the Son is an antichrist. (1 John 2:22)

The third passage is found in Paul's letter to the Thessalonian church. Second Thessalonians 2 describes the man of lawlessness. Many Christians assume this is the same person as the beast in Revelation. I am almost entirely convinced it's not. The beast was someone in the past. The man of lawlessness seems to be someone in the future.

> For that day will not come until there is a great rebellion against God and the man of lawlessness is revealed—the one who brings destruction. He will exalt himself and defy everything that people

call god and every object of worship. He will even sit in the temple of God, claiming that he himself is God. (2 Thess 2:3–4)

The man of lawlessness will sit in the temple. What is the temple? We are. Paul writes in 1 Corinthians that the Christian church is the temple, not the Jerusalem temple. In other words, this man will claim to be a Christian. Paul continues,

For this lawlessness is already at work secretly, and it will remain secret until the one who is holding it back steps out of the way. Then the man of lawlessness will be revealed. (2 Thess 2:7–9)

The Holy Spirit is today advancing the gospel all over the world, but someday, right before Jesus returns, the Holy Spirit will step out of the way and let him loose. But the Lord Jesus will slay him with the breath of his mouth and destroy him by the splendor of his coming. So it seems to me that the man of lawlessness is either the antichrist or he is an antichrist. What does this passage tell us about him? God is restraining the man of lawlessness by the preaching of the gospel. As long as Christianity is growing, and it will relentlessly, the antichrist is bound. But even when he's unbound, what will save us from him? The return of Christ will rescue the world from the attacks of antichrists.

The way we defeat antichrists is by following the true Christ. God is looking for loyal soldiers to play their part. Could a politician be an antichrist? Yes. Could that preacher be an antichrist? Yes. But we defeat them by preaching the true Christ. As we live out our faith openly and fearlessly, we align ourselves with the victorious King. By staying true to his teachings and spreading his message, we actively counter the deception and influence of the man of lawlessness. The fear of terrifying end-time predictions should not drive us to isolation. Scripture calls us to engage with the world, to be a light, and to trust in God's sovereign plan.

This world is fading away, along with everything that people crave. But anyone who does what pleases God will live forever. (1 John 2:17)

Our identity in Christ calls us to rise above fear and to trust in his plan. We are to be active participants in his mission, not passive spectators cowering in fear. The challenges we face, including the presence of antichrists, are opportunities for us to demonstrate our faith and commitment to Christ.

When we encounter fear, whether it is provoked by politicians, preachers, or world events, we should remember that our strength lies in our unity with Christ and his ultimate victory. Our focus should be on spreading the gospel, engaging with our communities, and living out the values that Jesus taught. This proactive approach not only fortifies our faith but also serves as a beacon of hope and truth in a world often overshadowed by fear and uncertainty.

Let's commit to being lights in the world, confidently proclaiming the gospel and living in a manner that reflects our true identity in Christ. As we live courageously and faithfully, we not only overcome our fears but also inspire others to do the same. Our ultimate hope and security are found in Jesus Christ, who has overcome the world. By following him, we play our part in his grand plan, shining brightly in a world that desperately needs the light of Christ.

Reflect: Are you tempted to fear the events leading up to the return of Jesus, or are you confident in his plan for the future of his church?

42

The Money Test

Accompanying Scripture Reading: Mark 12:38–44

IN A WORLD FIXATED on accumulating wealth and possessions, Jesus offers a counter-cultural teaching: to store our treasures in heaven. This principle is vividly illustrated in Mark 12:41–44, where Jesus contrasts the offerings of the rich with the humble gift of a poor widow. She gave two small coins, which was everything she had, demonstrating extravagant generosity and complete trust in God's provision. Jesus celebrated her sacrifice, highlighting that true generosity isn't measured by the size of the gift, but by the portion of our wealth we are willing to give back to God:

> Jesus called his disciples to him and said, "I tell you the truth, this poor widow has given more than all the others who are making contributions. For they gave a tiny part of their surplus, but she, poor as she is, has given everything she had to live on." (Mark 12:43–44)

THE LIFE

This widow's story teaches us that our sanctification leads to sacrificial generosity, reflecting the heart of Jesus who gave everything for us.

A few years ago, my son Lincoln and I were playing in our front yard when he told me, "I have good news, and I have bad news. The bad news is, we're gonna have to excavate your house. The good news is . . . you got a package!" Usually, when we receive good and bad news, they are not equally impactful. When it comes to wealth, there's good news and bad news. The good news is we are rich. Compared to most humans throughout history, we are crazy rich. If you have access to a car, a phone, or modern entertainment of any kind, you are crazy rich. The bad news is we are rich. Wealth can distract us from our dependence on God. The pursuit of more can consume us, making it harder to enter the kingdom of God.

> It is easier for a camel to go through the eye of a needle than for a rich person to enter the Kingdom of God! (Mark 10:25)

Why is it difficult for a rich person to join God's forever family? Because the pursuit of money takes all of our attention. Marketers make you think that what you don't have is what you need. We are tempted to focus on our lack rather than our blessings, but happiness is found in contentment. God tells us that he will supply all of our needs while we follow him. This promise allows us to focus on what really matters while he takes care of the rest. God is omnipotent. He can take care of the small details and the most important details simultaneously, but focusing on insignificant details distracts from important details.

In addition, focusing on temporary pleasure leaves a hole in our lives that cannot be filled by anything physical, and as we attempt to fill a spiritual hole with physical assets, we develop addictions to physical assets. Consumeristic addictions lead to overconsumption and gluttony. If you're reading this, you're rich, but because of the availability of loans, our pursuit of more can make us poor. An inability to delay gratification leads us to borrow from the future to fulfill the desires of the present.

Are you in debt? If yes, what is that debt costing you? What is it really costing you? Not just financially, but also emotionally and spiritually. You're rich. That's great, but be rich spiritually.

There's a biblical perspective on wealth that provides balance. Ecclesiastes 5:19 points out that wealth and the health to enjoy it are gifts from God. Our task is to recognize this gift and use it responsibly, not for self-indulgence, but to honor God and serve others.

The Money Test

> Teach those who are rich in this world not to be proud and not to trust in their money, which is so unreliable. Their trust should be in God, who richly gives us all we need for our enjoyment. (1 Tim 6:17)

Paul's advice to Timothy encapsulates the balance we need. Wealth isn't inherently evil; it's our attitude towards it and how we use it that matters. We are called to be rich in good works and generosity, storing up treasures in heaven through acts of kindness and love. Our reward is in heaven. Jesus promised great rewards for those who follow him faithfully, emphasizing this seventy-five times. Living generously is about investing in eternity.

Let's stop pursuing the fleeting riches of this world and focus on storing treasures in heaven. By living generously, we reflect the heart of Jesus and make an eternal impact. Our ultimate reward is not earthly accolades or comforts but in the eternal joy of seeing lives transformed for God's kingdom.

> Not that I was ever in need, for I have learned how to be content with whatever I have. I know how to live on almost nothing or with everything. I have learned the secret of living in every situation, whether it is with a full stomach or empty, with plenty or little. For I can do everything through Christ, who gives me strength. (Phil 4:11–13)

In the story of the widow's coins, Jesus didn't criticize the rich people for being rich, and he didn't necessarily criticize their generosity. Instead, he celebrated the extravagant generosity of the widow. She had incredible faith in God to provide for her. Jesus calculated the percentage of their generosity. It's not about the size of our gift. Jesus was teaching his disciples to do the math and calculate the percentage of their generosity. God trusted us with everything we have. He trusted us to do the right thing. Our sanctification leads us to extravagant generosity, and Jesus celebrates the moments that we give the way he gave, when we give sacrificially.

Reflect on your giving habits today. Generosity is a key indicator of spiritual health and maturity. Jesus often used money as a test of loyalty and commitment, and the money God has given you is a test, a test to grade your spiritual maturity.

Reflect: Are you tempted to pursue wealth for personal gain, or are you living generously?

43

Commune

Accompanying Scripture Reading: Matthew 26:17–30

IN THE GOSPELS, JESUS is often found at a table, sharing meals and fellowship with his disciples and others. These moments at the table were more than just eating together; they were opportunities for teaching, building relationships, and creating intentional community.

On the first day of the Festival of Unleavened Bread, the disciples came to Jesus and asked about where they would eat the Passover meal (Matt 26:17). Jesus instructed them to find a specific man in the city and prepare the meal at his house, and this preparation led to one of the most significant events in Christian history—the Last Supper.

As they gathered, Jesus revealed that one of the Twelve would betray him, causing great distress among the disciples. In this moment of tension,

Jesus continued to teach, using the bread and wine to offer them a new covenant:

> As they were eating, Jesus took some bread and blessed it. Then he broke it in pieces and gave it to the disciples, saying, "Take this and eat it, for this is my body." And he took a cup of wine and gave thanks to God for it. He gave it to them and said, "Each of you drink from it, for this is my blood, which confirms the covenant between God and his people. It is poured out as a sacrifice to forgive the sins of many." (Matt 26:26–28)

Jesus didn't die to start a religion. He died to start a relationship with us. This relationship is best described by the Greek word *koinonia*, which means participation in spiritual community or communion. In Matt 7:21–23, Jesus warns that not everyone who calls him "Lord" will enter the kingdom of heaven, but only those who do the will of his Father. This passage emphasizes the necessity of a genuine relationship with him. He's not asking for religious rituals. He's asking for our hearts.

One of the core aspects of Jesus' ministry was intentional community. Jesus focused on mentoring a few, who in turn mentored others. This created a ripple effect that changed the world. He mentored his disciples closely, showing them how to live and serve. This mentorship was hands-on and personal, often taking place around the table. As parents and leaders, we can emulate this by making our table time sacred, mentoring our children and others intentionally.

People often fail to recognize their need for community outside of a few key relationships. Most of us desire a relationship with our immediate family, a few friends, and a romantic partner, but we can't stop there. Communion is a statement of our intention to commune with God and each other. It's a commitment to make time for deep conversations, to ask meaningful questions, and to share life's fluctuations.

Today, we face many distractions that pull us away from genuine relationships. We have prioritized entertainment and convenience over meaningful interactions. Facebook friends are not friends unless you turn them into friends. Cell phones at the table can kill family dynamics and prevent us from engaging deeply with one another. Instead, we should use our table time to learn from others, to mentor, and to share our hearts.

Without close relationships, deep truths and core values are not passed from generation to generation, from family to family, or from community to community. If we have any humility at all, we learn from the people with whom we have relationships, and those lessons form our communities. The Christian growth plan is dependent on Christians leading other Christians. Discipleship and mentorship help us grow.

Do you have a mentor? If not, find one, then set a regular schedule of meetings. The meetings don't have to happen every week or even every month, but the time spent together should be intentional and relational. Ask your mentor thoughtful questions. Take notes. Ask for homework assignments. Take it seriously and let it form you.

The great command, to love God and love each other, is not simply a rule by which we live. It is the defining characteristic of who we are, and as we love God and love each other, we become more like God and more like each other.

The apostle Paul addressed the importance of community in his first letter to the Corinthians. He urged them to live in harmony and use the Lord's Supper to heal divisions (1 Cor 1:10; 11:18–22). Paul emphasized that genuine communion with God and each other transforms us, making us more like Christ and helping us to love one another. Jesus develops the best parts of us and quiets our selfish and anxious thoughts.

Jesus created us. He put everything in us that we would need to do the things he called us to do. However, because we were born into a sinful world, those qualities and gifts often need to be developed, to be called out of us. Jesus often used questions to teach and engage with his followers. He asked 307 questions in the Gospels, using them to foster reflection and learning. This method of teaching is powerful because it encourages introspection and personal growth.

We are then called to serve others the way Jesus served us, to call out the gifts that God has given to our Christian brothers and sisters. Jesus calls us to move from being sheep to shepherds. This transition calls us to mentor someone else as we take responsibility for our own spiritual growth. Everyone should have a mentor and also mentor someone else. The key is to not wait for perfection but to start leading others where we are.

Who are you mentoring? Will you make a commitment to build relationships that reflect the love and grace of Christ, to disciple others the way Jesus is discipling you? The impact of a life is measured by how much it is given away. Jesus, as the ultimate shepherd, gave his life for us and calls us to shepherd others. Just as Jesus used the table to teach and build relationships, let's use our tables to do the same. Make it a priority to commune with other believers at the table, to celebrate the Last Supper by serving someone who is one or two steps behind you in the spiritual growth journey.

Reflect: Have you made communion, both at church and at home with friends and family, a priority in your life?

44

Homecoming

Accompanying Scripture Reading: Matthew 26:36–56

WHEN YOU PICTURE HOME, what do you see? Is the house small or big? A trailer or a mansion? When you think of home, do you think of a town or a farm, a building or a room? A more important question is, do you see places, or do you see faces? Do you have fond memories of times around the table, in the kitchen, or the yard? Or are your thoughts clouded by anger, by fear, or regret? Are your memories of home loving or lonely, happy or hard? The good news is, no matter how you answer these questions, there is hope for healing and joy because as long as you live in this world, your picture of home is not complete. You can choose to fill in the blank space with more of the same or with better times with more grace. The truth is, if you're God's child, this world is not your home. Your home is with your

Homecoming

Heavenly Father. It is a place of beauty and fun, of joy and love. Our future is truly a homecoming. Our home is coming. God is bringing heaven here.

Imagine this: You have just completed a two-week road trip to visit your in-laws, and you are driving home. You're about an hour away, and you are desperate. You think, "Are we almost there? Are we almost home?" What do you want so desperately? You want your bed. You want your recliner, your shower, and pink luffa. You just want to be home!

Why do we say, "There's no place like home?" It's because there is rest available to us at home that's not available anywhere else. At home you can really relax. You can totally be yourself, walk around in your underwear, make all kinds of embarrassing sounds, and wear those old, ratty sweatpants your wife won't let you wear out of the house. But we can't stay there. We have to go to work. We have to get the kids to practice and the dog to the vet. We have to go to every store in town because the ramen noodles are sold out at every grocery store. Then there's the bank, the gym, that meeting at the school, and we've got to do something about that rash. There's so much to do, and we just get weary.

Have you ever felt weary? I mean really weary, burnt out, frustrated with life, sick of the job? Have you ever thought, "The kids are wearing me down. I can't do it anymore." Did you know Jesus felt like that? One time, the night before he was killed, Jesus was so exhausted and overwhelmed that his body began to shut down. He sweated drops of blood, so he asked his disciples to pray. Then he prayed. Why was he so distressed? He knew it was time. He knew that soon he would be killed.

> [Jesus] told them "My soul is crushed with grief to the point of death. Stay here and keep watch with me." "My Father! If it is possible, let this cup of suffering be taken away from me. Yet I want your will to be done, not mine." Then he returned to the disciples and found them asleep. He said to Peter, "Couldn't you watch with me even one hour?" (Matt 26:38–40)

Jesus asked his disciples to stay awake and pray with him three times before he finally quit asking them. He let his disciples get some rest. Jesus and his disciples were exhausted. They had traveled all over Israel. They were ridiculed because of the statements Jesus was making. The glee of witnessing lives being changed and bodies being healed was exciting, but exhausting. In addition, they had just eaten the Passover meal. That's a big meal. I don't know about you, but when I eat a big meal, I get tired. The meal also included quite a bit of wine. That, too, can make you tired.

Maybe that's why Jesus washed his disciples' feet in that upper room. He knew they were tired and weary from their travels. After Jesus washed their feet, he delivered some encouraging words. He reminded them that they would never experience complete rest until they were home in heaven, a home that would be bigger and better than anything they could possibly imagine.

> "Don't let your hearts be troubled. Trust in God, and trust also in me. There is more than enough room in my Father's home. If this were not so, would I have told you that I am going to prepare a place for you? When everything is ready, I will come and get you, so that you will always be with me where I am. And you know the way to where I am going." "No, we don't know, Lord," Thomas said. "We have no idea where you are going, so how can we know the way?" Jesus told him, "I am the way, the truth, and the life. No one can come to the Father except through me." (John 14:1–6)

This is a description of our homecoming. God is building a mansion for each of us, and someday he's going to bring us to them. All your Christian family members who have died will be there. Your Christian friends will be there, and because God will be there, we, too, will be there.

Jesus is the way. If you're trying to get to heaven any other way, you won't make it. We could never get to heaven on our own. We are not strong enough, but Jesus bought it for us. He built a home for us, and he made a way for us to get there.

So, what about you? There is a home in heaven for you, but there's only one way there. Give your life to Jesus Christ. Make him your Lord. He built you a home in heaven, then he died on a cross so your sins could be forgiven, and that forgiveness is the key to your eternal home. Jesus is the key. So take the key. It's the greatest gift ever given. Someday heaven will come to earth, and all things will be made new. Will you be at home here?

Not long ago, after church, my six-year-old son asked, "Dad, if the soldiers killed Jesus, then he rose from the dead, why didn't he kill the soldiers who killed him?" I said, "Jesus died so he could forgive people for sinning, and the first people he forgave were the people who killed him."

> Jesus said, "Father, forgive them, for they do not know what they are doing." (Luke 23:34)

If you have received God's forgiveness, you are a child of God, and you will live in his kingdom forever. He has built you a forever home, and because you have chosen to trust him to save you, rather than attempting to earn salvation, your eternity with him is secure. Today, spend some time attempting to imagine heaven.

Reflect: What will it be like when you see your Christian family and friends in heaven?

45

Who to Vote For

Accompanying Scripture Reading: John 18:28–40

WHO SHOULD WE VOTE for? It is very difficult to find a politician who aligns with all of our values and opinions and, unfortunately for just about all of us, a vote for yourself is a wasted vote. You can write your own name in, but that won't help the right candidate get elected. However, even though most people don't vote for themselves, they do vote selfishly. Most of us are tempted to vote based on who will help us personally or who will help people like us. We ask, "Who will fill my bank account and make me more comfortable?"

For a Christian, this can't be one of our first questions in choosing a candidate. Christ would instruct us to vote selflessly for the candidate who will help the most possible people and for the agenda that will do the most possible good. Making that determination will include some education, investigation, and math. Most politicians claim their agenda will accomplish the most possible good, but an honest look often reveals otherwise.

Who to Vote For

After Jesus' baptism, while he prayed in the wilderness, the devil offered to give him control of the whole world. I am sure Jesus was tempted to take that control, to end the division in congress, to stop the rioting, to end the hunger, and defeat injustice. Wouldn't it be great if Syria and North Korea bowed to the authority of Jesus? Wouldn't we love it if China and America were led by the instructions of Jesus? We would all love to vote for Jesus in the next election, but we also know offers like this offer from the devil often come with a catch. In this story, the devil demanded that Jesus worship him in order to gain that power. We also know that the devil offered Jesus something he couldn't give, but temptations are often unrealistic. We fantasize about having things we cannot possibly have, and those fantasies lead us to make terrible decisions. It's like the United States government borrowing money from China to pay its debt to China.

> "Get out of here, Satan," Jesus told him. "For the Scriptures say, 'You must worship the Lord your God and serve only him.'" (Matt 4:10)

The good news is, Jesus rejected the devil's temptation, and so can we. When we are offered power, we are tempted to forget that power will always come with consequences, good or bad. It's easier to play god than to be God.

Jesus knew love had the power to do what power could not. With power you can force someone to do something, but only love can build a healthy relationship. That is one reason Jesus never used his power to force us to love him. Jesus came as a defenseless child, to live amongst us in servanthood, and that kind of love started a movement that physical dominance never could have.

> If my people who are called by my name will humble themselves and pray and seek my face and turn from their wicked ways, I will hear from heaven and will forgive their sins and restore their land. (2 Chr 7:14)

Selfish politics uses power for personal gain. How do you get a dog to obey you? You teach it that you are in charge. You stand over it in discipline.

Selfish politics uses power to impress. If I can get people clapping for me, they'll follow me, and self-righteousness starts to puff up. This is what causes people to ignorantly follow the political opinions of celebrities and athletes.

Selfish politics uses victimhood to control. Our society has glorified victimhood. I'm not talking about real victims. I'm talking about fakers.

The Life

They whine us into submission, but that's a short-term strategy. It doesn't work in the long-term. Victimhood is never a victory.

After Jesus was arrested, he stood before Pilate who would determine his fate.

> Pilate... called for Jesus to be brought to him. "Are you the king of the Jews?" he asked him. Jesus replied, "Is this your own question, or did others tell you about me?" "Am I a Jew?" Pilate retorted. "Your own people and their leading priests brought you to me for trial. Why? What have you done?" Jesus answered, "My Kingdom is not an earthly kingdom. If it were, my followers would fight to keep me from being handed over to the Jewish leaders. But my Kingdom is not of this world." (John 18:33–38)

Pilate wanted to know if Jesus was using his power for leverage over people or if Jesus was innocent. He wanted to know if Jesus was a victim, but Jesus chose not to play the victim card. He wasn't a victim. He wasn't weak. He could have destroyed all of Rome's soldiers with a snap. Pilate expected a power play, but Jesus didn't do it.

> [Pilate] asked [Jesus], "Where are you from?" But Jesus gave no answer. "Why don't you talk to me?" Pilate demanded. Don't you realize that I have the power to release you or crucify you? Then Jesus said, "You would have no power over me at all unless it were given to you from above." (John 19:9–11)

Pilate boasted about his power, but it didn't do for him what he wanted it to do. The irony is that Pilate had some power, but he was living in fear, fear of the mob, fear of Caesar, fear of a revolution. It seemed like Jesus had no power, but he was not controlled by fear.

Christians, we've been fighting with the wrong kind of power. I won't tell you which bubble to fill in on your ballot in the next election, but I will tell you to vote for people who are truly victims, vote for the outcast, for the marginalized, and for the poor. Your vote gives you some power. So, vote for love.

> If you help the poor, you are lending to the Lord—and he will repay you! (Prov 19:17)

To participate in democratic elections, we have to pick our battles. Because there will never be a politician that will agree with us 100 percent of the time, we have to decide which issues will affect our voting decisions.

Here are four ways that voters pick a candidate:

1. Personalities: Many voters ignore the issues and vote for the candidate they like most. That's how Hitler had so much power.
2. Group Think: Most voters simply follow the crowd. They vote for the candidate their friends vote for to avoid extra work or ruffling feathers. The problem is that the crowd is often wrong. The crowd shouted, "Crucify him."
3. Amount of Agreement: Some people vote for the candidate with whom they agree most often. This method isn't bad, but it's not the best.
4. Issue Prioritization: The best way to vote is to determine which issues are most important and, within reason, vote for the person who is on the right side of the most important issues.

Some political issues are very important. Others are distractions. Can you imagine being Jesus in our world trying to decide who to vote for? Jesus knew the truth on every issue, but he only chose to fight for a few issues. He prioritized. I bet Jesus had an opinion about taxes, but when the religious leaders asked him to give his opinion, he just told them to pay their taxes. When everyone wanted him to become a political activist, he wouldn't do it. Jesus was surprisingly silent on the political issues of the day. He just told them to obey the government leaders. Then he put spiritual matters above it all. We have to put the most important things first. Jesus seized his moment by neglecting earthly politics. Don't give yourself to the most popular political issues of the day just because that's what the news likes to talk about.

We are tempted to spend more time squandering our moment and criticizing people than savoring our moment and thanking God for the time we live in and the mission we've been given. We're so angry that our political leaders don't govern the way we think they should that we get distracted from what really matters. As a result, we make the politicians our enemies, but they are not our enemy. They are often sick people in need of a hospital. They are lost people in need of Jesus.

When the church constantly nags the government, protesting and canceling, our voice is muffled. Eventually, they will start to ignore us. Then, if the Christians have no voice at all, we will be left with a totally depraved world.

In Europe, some forms of opposition to abortion are considered hate speech. America isn't there yet, but if we keep talking like we hate everyone and everything with whom we disagree, the world will start labeling more of our opinions as "hate speech." We must pick our battles. What if Christians became so known for their desire to love and care for as many people as possible that we changed our reputation from purveyors of hate speech to purveyors of love speech. Love speech. That's our language. Let's prioritize issues that will show love and care for the most people possible.

Rise above political disagreements and talk about what will do the most good for our world, not for us, but for the people we've been called to love.

Reflect: When you think about who you should vote for, do you think more about how the election will affect you or how it will affect others?

46

Wear Christian T-Shirts

Accompanying Scripture Reading: Matthew 26:57–68

MORE THAN 60 PERCENT of born-again Christians in America between the ages of 18 and 39 believe Jesus is not the only path to salvation.[1] We've developed a consumeristic version of Christianity that says, "My faith is all about me, but if it's not your cup of tea, you can pick a different religion." As a result, evangelism is becoming outdated. In fact, almost half of practicing Christian millennials say evangelism is wrong.[2] Our biblical mandate is to lead people to Jesus, but we are following the opinions of culture, not the truth of Scripture.

> Don't copy the behavior and customs of this world, but let God transform you into a new person by changing the way you think.

1. Kumar, "60% of Adults under 40."
2. Barna Group, "Almost Half."

> Then you will learn to know God's will for you, which is good and pleasing and perfect. (Rom 12:2)

Think about the storage room in your house. You've got one box for the clothes your kids grew out of, one for old photo albums, one for your wedding dress, and one for Christmas decorations. Who am I kidding? This is America, you've got five for Christmas decorations. When Christmas comes around, you pull out the boxes with the decorations, use them for a month, then put them away.

This is what we tend to do with our faith. We put our faith in one of our boxes, but we have a lot of boxes. When Sunday comes around, we pull out our Christian box, do the Christian stuff, then hide it away for the rest of the week so we can pull out the other things that are important to us. "I pull this box out on Mondays for work, this one on Tuesdays, this one on Wednesdays, and the dirty box is for Fridays. That's the fun box. It smells bad, and I hope my wife never looks in it, or God, but I enjoy that box. Well, kind of. I enjoy it while it's open, but when I have to close it, I spend the rest of the week cleaning up the mess that it made. In fact, this box affects the rest of my week more than my Sunday box."

What's the one room in your house you never show guests? The storage room. This stuff just hides in there. Do you store your Christianity in a box so you can just pull it out when you need it? Or do you wear your faith everywhere you go? Are you willing to wear a Christian T-shirt on Fridays? Christians, have you gone public with your faith, or are you afraid of awkward conversations? Are you living to bring glory to God? Or are you living to bring glory to yourself? You might say something like, "I swear too much. I can't tell everyone I'm a Christian." Or, "I don't want to put a Christian bumper sticker on my car. I cut people off in traffic." Well, stop it. You've got a mission. You've got a calling on your life, and those things that are keeping you from leading people to Jesus are holding you back.

Consider Peter's story. When Jesus was arrested, Peter followed Jesus and the soldiers at a distance, and eventually denied three times that he knew Jesus. Why did Peter deny knowing Jesus? Was he scared? Was he mad because Jesus made him put the sword away in the garden? Was he doubting Jesus was the Messiah? To answer this, we should look at a story that happened a few months before this event.

Jesus began to tell the disciples that the Son of Man must suffer many terrible things. Peter took Jesus aside and reprimanded him for saying such things. Jesus turned around, looked at his disciples, and then reprimanded Peter.

Peter trusted Jesus when he thought he was on the way to the throne. Peter wanted power, but now that it appeared Jesus had lost, Peter doubted Jesus. Peter wanted life to get easier, not harder. Jesus never promised to make life easier. Maybe you started following Jesus because you thought he would make life easier, but then realized he wouldn't. Jesus will make your life better, not easier. When you realize that, it will offend you. You, too, will be tempted to turn away from Jesus.

Eventually, this change of thinking needs to happen to every Christian. We stop seeing our lives the way the world sees their lives, and we start to realize we were created for something better than the pleasures of this world. That's the transition we see Peter going through here. Jesus had to offend Peter's way of thinking so Peter would begin to fully become the unashamed, passionate leader of the church that God created him to be.

Peter did deny Jesus, and when he realized what he did, he was emotionally broken.

> Peter left the courtyard, weeping bitterly. (Luke 22:62)

Jesus, however, did not leave Peter in this dejected state. After Jesus rose from the dead, he sought out Peter to reconcile. Like the Shepherd going after the lost sheep, Jesus went after Peter. That is when Peter had an incredible encounter with Jesus on a Galilean beach (John 21). Peter denied knowing Jesus three times, then three times Jesus asked Peter "Do you love me?" Three times Peter said, "Yes," and three times Jesus told Peter to feed his sheep.

After Jesus rose from the dead on the third day, Peter repented three times. Jesus led Peter through a process of renewing his mind, and he traded his shame for faith. We see Peter again in the book of Acts, preaching boldly about his faith in Jesus, and many people were saved:

> Those who believed what Peter said were baptized and added to the church that day—about 3,000 in all. (Acts 2:41)

Peter invited people to repent. To repent literally means to "change your mind." He invited people to stop seeing things their way and start seeing things God's way. With this message, three thousand people were saved. By this time, Peter had reached a new level of faith maturity. Eventually, Peter was killed for his faith. They crucified him upside down.

What about you? Have you repented of your way and put your faith in God's way?

I am not ashamed of this Good News about Christ. (Rom 1:16)

Don't follow Jesus because it's easy or because you want to sit on a throne. Follow Jesus because you want to bow to his throne.

Reflect: Are you unashamed of your Christian mission, or are there people in your community who are unaware of your faith?

47

But God Can

Accompanying Scripture Reading: Matthew 27:20–31

TODAY WE'RE REFLECTING ON the horrific torture Jesus endured before he died. Matthew 27 recounts how Pilate ordered Jesus to be flogged with a lead-tipped whip before handing him over to be crucified. The governor's soldiers mocked Jesus, dressing him in a scarlet robe, placing a crown of thorns on his head, and striking him repeatedly. This passage emphasizes the brutal treatment Jesus faced as the entire regiment beat him until they were too tired to continue. Jesus endured unimaginable suffering on the cross, and in his humanity alone, he couldn't have done it.

Let's ask two questions of Jesus' crucifixion:

1. How did Jesus endure the cross?

The Life

Everyone has felt the urge to quit at some point. We all face moments of doubt. "I'm not smart enough. No one will help me. I don't have enough money. I'm too shy. I'm too ugly." Maybe you want to quit your marriage or job. Quitting is easy and perseverance is hard. You might have to work harder or fail more than others. You might have to be more disciplined. You might not be as smart, pretty, or wealthy, but God has given you everything you need to do what he created you to do. Do the best you can with what God has given you, and it will be enough.

There have been many days I wanted to quit my job. I think, "I'm not a good enough preacher. People keep leaving! I can't remember your names!" After four failed IVF attempts, my wife and I wanted to quit trying to have children, but we are so glad we did a fifth IVF. Our two sons are pretty happy about it too.

All through Scripture God asks people to do things, and they make excuses for why they can't. He gives a command, and they respond with, "But I . . ."

God wanted Moses to lead the Israelites out of Egypt and speak God's words to Pharaoh, and Moses said, "But I am slow of speech" (Exod 4:10). God asked Gideon to go to the Midianites, and Gideon said, "But I am the least in my entire family" (Judg 6:15). God asked Jeremiah to be a prophet, and Jeremiah said, "But I am too young!" (Jer 1:6). God asked Esther to deliver his people, and she said, "But I have not been called to go to the king" (Esth 4:11). God wanted to make Abraham into a great nation, and he said, "But I'm too old" (Gen 17:17). Jesus told Peter to cast the nets on the other side of the boat, and he said, "But I already tried" (Luke 5:1–11). And in each of these stories, the reader wants God to say, "You can do it!" But he didn't. Instead, God turned the focus away from the person and onto himself.

The city of Corinth was a thriving Roman city, the New York City of the first century. They had a saying in Corinth, "none but the tough could survive."[1] Yet, in this city, there was a group of unskilled, uneducated people who started a movement that amazed everyone: the Christian church. In their struggle you'd assume Paul would write to praise them. Instead, he talked about their inadequacies. A lot of the people leading this church were poor or even slaves, but Paul didn't lower his expectations. Instead, he pointed out their weaknesses:

---

1. Guzik, "Study Guide for Acts 18."

But God Can

> Brothers and sisters, think of what you were when you were called. Not many of you were wise by human standards; not many were influential; not many were of noble birth. But God chose the foolish things of the world to shame the wise; God chose the weak things of the world to shame the strong. (1 Cor 1:26–27)

We make excuses for why we can't do what God wants us to do, but it was never our strength we should have been relying on.

> Therefore, as it is written: "Let the one who boasts boast in the Lord." (1 Cor 1:31)

We're tempted to say, "But I can't do it. I'm not wise. I'm not popular." The truth is, God is bigger than your "but." Instead of saying, "But I . . ." Scripture says, "But God." Those words will change your life. I'm not good enough, but God is!

> My health may fail, and my spirit may grow weak, but God remains the strength of my heart. (Ps 73:26)

Joseph said to his brothers who sold him into slavery, "You intended to harm me, but God intended it all for good" (Gen 50:20). Jesus said, "Humanly speaking, it is impossible. But with God everything is possible" (Matt 19:26).

How can we be good enough? How can we handle the pain? How can we face the problems? We can't, but God can. God can do more through us than we could ever do in ourselves! He gives us strength.

> [The Lord] said, "My grace is all you need. My power works best in weakness." So now I am glad to boast about my weaknesses, so that the power of Christ can work through me. (2 Cor 12:9)

How did Jesus endure the cross? In his humanity, he couldn't, but God did.

The second question is about Christ's intentions.

2. Why did Jesus endure the cross?

What did Jesus' death accomplish? First, he won a spiritual victory over the spiritual world.

> In this way, he disarmed the spiritual rulers and authorities. He shamed them publicly by his victory over them on the cross. (Col 2:15)

The Life

In the Old Testament, we see an evil partnership between humans and spirits in Babylon, in Egypt, and throughout the Old Testament that isn't possible today. Jesus took their power. The last thing Jesus said before he ascended to heaven was a description of this reality:

> I have been given all authority in heaven and on earth. (Matt 28:18)

Second, Jesus endured the cross to give us resurrection. We use the word "gospel" when we talk about Jesus' death and resurrection. "Gospel" means "good news." Jesus' death is good news.

There's a difference between good advice and good news. We're tempted to turn the gospel into good advice, a list of rules we need to follow or wise advice for living in this world, but that is a weak version of the gospel. Good advice is a teacher telling her students to study for the test. She says, "If you do the homework and read the book, you'll do fine on the test." That's good advice, but what if the teacher said, "Scoot over. I'll take the test for you." That's good news, and that's what Jesus did on the cross. We were supposed to die for our sins, but he died for us. That student did not deserve to have the teacher take his test for him, but the teacher did it anyway. That is called substitutionary atonement. Religious-minded people don't like it. They think this kind of gift gives people license to sin. That's what Paul emphasizes after laying out the good news in Rom 6:

> Well then, should we keep on sinning so that God can show us more and more of his wonderful grace? Of course not! Since we have died to sin, how can we continue to live in it? (Rom 6:1)

After he shared the good news, he had to clarify that we shouldn't react to the good news by doing whatever we want. If our flesh still controlled us, we would use our flesh for selfish reasons. If my heart's desire is to get human pleasure, I will use the gospel to satisfy my flesh. However, if I surrender to God, I am living with a renewed mind. When my "But I" mindset changes to a "But God" mindset, Jesus sanctifies us. If we don't teach in such a way that people respond with, "But that doesn't seem fair," then I haven't actually shared the good news. The beauty of God's grace is that it isn't fair.

When humans hear about God's gift, it should sound too good to be true, but not all good news is easy news. Good news could be that you got a new job, but that's not a promise that the job will be easy.

> If any of you wants to be my follower, you must give up your own way, take up your cross, and follow me. (Matt 16:24)

Jesus didn't die so we can live in this world. Jesus died so we could die with the promise of resurrection. The good news requires death. The old self must die, but the new self is better. Imagine owning the whole world: Apple, Google, America . . . the Kansas City Chiefs! Jesus said that power would actually be bad for us.

> But [God] said to me, "My grace is sufficient for you, for my power is made perfect in weakness." Therefore I will boast all the more gladly about my weaknesses, so that Christ's power may rest on me. That is why, for Christ's sake, I delight in weaknesses, in insults, in hardships, in persecutions, in difficulties. For when I am weak, then I am strong. (2 Cor 12:9–10)

Trade your "But I" excuses for "But God" empowerment. You're not who you used to be. You are a new creation. The old is gone. When I am weak, God in me is strong. Jesus' death and resurrection should give you hope that you can endure anything in this world because you know this world isn't your home.

Reflect: Identify a few areas where you're tempted to focus on your own weakness instead of relying on God's strength.

48

God's Approval

Accompanying Scripture Reading: Luke 23:26–43

CRUCIFIXION WAS NOT ONLY intended to be a brutally painful form of capital punishment, it was also meant to humiliate people and scare others into good behavior. As Jesus hung naked, mangled, and deformed on the cross, he demonstrated his incredible power. He did this not with physical strength, but through grace and perseverance. It is that strength that impressed one of the criminals hanging next to Jesus on a cross:

> One of the criminals hanging beside [Jesus] scoffed, "So you're the Messiah, are you? Prove it by saving yourself—and us, too, while you're at it!" But the other criminal protested, "Don't you fear God even when you have been sentenced to die? We deserve to die for our crimes, but this man hasn't done anything wrong." Then he said, "Jesus, remember me when you come into your Kingdom." And

> Jesus replied, "I assure you, today you will be with me in paradise."
> (Luke 23:39–43)

No one admired the criminals hanging on the crosses beside Jesus. They had absolutely nothing to offer, and their time to reverse that painful reality had passed. Yet, when one criminal acknowledged Christ's lordship, Jesus saved him.

Do you know anyone who tries too hard to impress people? Have you ever seen a teenage girl taking selfies? She'll take countless selfies until she finds one she likes, then upload it to Instagram and think, "All in a day's work." Our world takes too many pictures. It's crazy. We have a terabyte of storage on our phones, and it's still not enough.

Young people take a lot of pictures because they care about their appearance. Older people take a lot because they can't believe it's free. When I was younger, we had to be selective with our pictures. We'd take thirty-six pictures, wait for them to be developed, and discover that most were unusable. Today, pictures are free and instant, allowing us to take multiple shots of our food at a restaurant. We try every angle to make sure we impress as many people as possible.

Imagine pleasing everyone. Think about the people upset with you suddenly being pleased. Imagine that no matter what you do, everyone thinks you're awesome. It sounds ridiculous because it is. It's impossible. On the other hand, imagine pleasing God. That seems like a more difficult task, but it's not. How could a perfect God be pleased with flawed humans? God can be pleased with us the same way parents are pleased with their children. And if God is pleased with me, why do I try so hard to please people?

This is the problem with most religion. Almost all religions are works-based, including a lot of Christian teaching. We naturally believe we must be good enough to earn God's approval, but Christianity is not that kind of religion. Works-based religion is called legalism, and legalism does not impress God because it leads to pride.

Jesus was good for us because we couldn't be good. The Israelites tried for millennia, and now we're trying. Our efforts will fail. The gospel is called good news because God is good, not because we are good, and he has offered to give us his goodness.

> God saved you by his grace when you believed. And you can't take credit for this; it is a gift from God. Salvation is not a reward for

the good things we have done, so none of us can boast about it. (Eph 2:8–9)

If I could earn my salvation or be good enough to keep it, I would have something to be prideful about. But I can't. The thief on the cross did nothing good, but he's in heaven. If you add up all your good and bad behavior, you will always get a negative number. We deserve hell. That's why the prophet Isaiah says all our good deeds are like filthy rags compared to the goodness God requires (Isa 64:5–6).

We want to be able to earn our salvation because then we would have something to boast about. We think, "I don't drink, smoke, chew, or go with girls who do. Look how great I am." We need a savior. We can't save ourselves. We are drowning and can't swim. We're in prison without a key or even a spoon with which to dig. We're stranded on an island with no boat or trees. The good news is our savior came.

The fastest way to forget what God thinks about you is to be consumed with what people think about you. Your Heavenly Father knows your flaws and loves you unconditionally, but we spend so much time trying to impress people who don't love us. We're all comparing, trying to impress people and be better than others, but comparison kills community. If you want to see a miserable group, find people trying to one-up each other. That's what the Pharisees did.

Pharisees were known as the "Separated Ones."[1] They judged the world and separated themselves by doing a little better. They made up rules about how to act, eat, and dress. Initially, their goal was to worship God, but they ended up worshiping themselves. They felt holy by obeying their made-up rules, but they weren't holy because they should have compared themselves to God, who is perfect.

Paul, an ex-Pharisee, said in Gal 1:10 that he was not trying to win the approval of people but of God. If pleasing people was Paul's goal, he would not have been a Christian. Today, it might be popular to call yourself a Christian, but not back then. To follow Christ, Paul had to become an outcast. His old friends hated him.

Human reasoning says, "I'm better than most, so I deserve more than most." Human reasoning tries to be fair, but God's grace isn't fair. It's all about Jesus, not us. Peter, speaking to religious leaders, declared that salvation is found in no one else but Jesus. This bold proclamation amazed the

---

1. Zavada, "Who Were the Pharisees?"

leaders, who then commanded the apostles never to speak or teach in the name of Jesus again, but Peter and John couldn't stop:

> We cannot stop telling about everything we have seen and heard.
> (Acts 4:20)

We obey God rather than men, not to earn his approval but because he gives approval even when we don't deserve it. That's why Peter and John couldn't stop talking about it. It was that good.

Did you grow up in a church that said it believed in grace but convinced you that you weren't good enough to earn or keep it? Do you still think you can be good enough? You can't, but Jesus can. And he was. The only way to be good enough is by letting him be good enough for you.

Jesus was perfect, and that intimidated the Pharisees. So rather than follow Jesus, they rejected Jesus. They wanted people admiring them, not admiring Jesus. They could compare themselves to everyone else and feel like they won, but not to Jesus. If anyone could have earned salvation, it would have been the Pharisees. But Paul left the Pharisees to follow Jesus, recognizing that the best of Pharisaical obedience is filthy rags.

> As for me, may I never boast about anything except the cross of our Lord Jesus Christ. Because of that cross, my interest in this world has been crucified, and the world's interest in me has also died. (Gal 6:14)

Don't seek the approval of people. Seek the approval of God. Declare he is your Lord and follow him.

Reflect: How would your life change if you focused more on pleasing God and less on pleasing people?

49

Play Infinite Games

Accompanying Scripture Reading: Luke 23:43-49

WHEN JESUS DIED ON the cross, it appeared he had lost. People went back to their normal lives and assumed Jesus was just another fake messiah, but Jesus had a bigger plan. He was playing the long game.

> Then Jesus shouted, "Father, I entrust my spirit into your hands!"
> And with those words he breathed his last. (Luke 23:46)

What gets your endorphins firing? Maybe it's the stock market, movies, books, sports, sex, drugs, or alcohol. The problem with these stimulants is that the more we use these things to feel an emotional high, the harder it becomes to achieve that excitement. Over time, it takes more and more to get the same rush, leading to a depressing cycle. The solution is to stop living in pursuit of those feelings. That's easier said than done, but the way

Play Infinite Games

to stop living for a temporary feeling is to start living for something bigger than yourself.

The happy feelings you will experience in heaven will far outweigh anything you can feel on earth, making it worth delaying gratification. However, that requires us to see the eternal nature of our lives. James Carse, a professor at New York University, identified two kinds of games humans play: finite games and infinite games.[1] Finite games, like sports, have a beginning, an end, and a clear winner. These games have known players, clear boundaries, and rules, making them easy for us to understand and enjoy, at least for a while. Modern sports are the clearest example of this kind of game, and the greatest evidence that sports are finite is that referees now stop games to review plays to ensure everything is fair and the winner deserves to win.

Infinite games, however, are less familiar. In these games, the rules change, there are known and unknown players, and the goal is to keep playing. There's no clear ending, and you don't know who wins, which can be frustrating.

The church is in an infinite game, but often acts like it's in a finite game. We think, "If we can just get more people on Sunday mornings than the church down the street, we'll be happy." But God called us to a different game. We are part of an infinite game that didn't start with us and won't end with us. If your goal is to find the bad guys in Christianity and separate from those who disagree with you, you're playing a finite game. Instead, we should continually point people to Jesus. Our goal is to lead more people to Jesus, and we will never see the end of that mission. We are part of an eternal story of God creating his family.

In Gen 22 we learn about Abraham, one of the most influential people in human history. God blessed him with a son, Isaac, through whom he planned to change the world. Then God tested Abraham's faith by asking him to sacrifice Isaac on an altar on Mount Moriah:

> Take your son, your only son—yes, Isaac, whom you love so much—and go to the land of Moriah. Go and sacrifice him as a burnt offering on one of the mountains, which I will show you. (Gen 22:2)

Abraham got up early the next morning without hesitation. He saddled his donkey and took two of his servants along with his beloved son, Isaac. After chopping the wood for the burnt offering, they set out for the

---

1. Carse, *Finite and Infinite Games*.

place God had instructed. On the third day of their journey, Abraham saw the place in the distance. Abraham placed the wood for the burnt offering on Isaac's shoulders, while he carried the fire and the knife. As they walked together, Isaac asked his dad where the sheep was for the burnt offering, and Abraham invited him to trust God:

> God will provide a sheep for the burnt offering, my son. (Gen 22:8)

When they arrived at the designated place, Abraham built an altar and arranged the wood on it. Then, in an act of profound obedience, he tied up his son, Isaac, and laid him on the altar atop the wood. Abraham picked up the knife to sacrifice his son, but at that very moment, the angel of the Lord stopped Abraham:

> "Don't lay a hand on the boy!" the angel said. "Do not hurt him in any way, for now I know that you truly fear God. You have not withheld from me even your son, your only son." (Gen 22:12)

Then Abraham looked up and saw a ram caught by its horns in a thicket. This ram became the substitute for Isaac, showing that God indeed provides.

Like Abraham, we are called to trust and obey, believing that God has a plan and will provide for us in every situation, but imagine being in Abraham's shoes. You've waited for a son your whole life, finally get one, and then God asks you to sacrifice him. Who do you love more? God or your son? This story foreshadows the crucifixion, when God gave his one and only Son. In fact, Mount Moriah is the same place where Jesus was crucified to cleanse us of our sins.

> For this is how God loved the world: he gave his one and only Son, so that everyone who believes in him will not perish but have eternal life. (John 3:16)

Moriah is not only where Jesus was crucified. It is also where the Jerusalem temple was built. In other words, things go to Mount Moriah to die so others can live. Isaac carried a cross up Mount Moriah 1,900 years before Jesus carried a cross up Mount Moriah, and who held the knife that was going to kill Isaac? Abraham. In a purely just world, God should be our executioner, but instead, he provided a substitute.

Isaac didn't know he was to be sacrificed, but Jesus willingly went to his death, knowing he was the Lamb of God. Romans killed Jesus, but they didn't overpower God. God orchestrated the whole event. Jesus carried the cross, but God held the knife, while planning a resurrection.

Play Infinite Games

We are like Isaac, meant to carry the cross, but Jesus took our place. Abraham trusted God because he was playing an infinite game. He didn't need to understand every step God asked him to take because he knew God had a plan. When you are in the midst of pain, fear, or doubt, remember that God has a plan, and Christ died for us. Our pain is finite, but our life is infinite. We have eternal life because God sacrificed his Son so we could live. At the right moment, the Lamb will appear and make all things right.

Our journey as Christians is filled with moments where we don't see the end, but we trust in God's greater plan. Consider the broader implications of playing an infinite game in your own life. It means focusing on long-term goals and values rather than immediate successes. It means understanding that our efforts today may not show results immediately, but they contribute to a larger purpose. Our mission is not just about filling pews or achieving short-term goals. Our mission is about nurturing a lasting faith, spreading the message of Jesus, and building a community that endures beyond our lifetimes.

We are tempted to seek validation from social media likes, career achievements, or material possessions. We think these will bring us happiness and fulfillment, but true fulfillment comes from playing the infinite game—living for something greater than ourselves, investing in relationships, and cultivating a mature faith in God. In the grand scheme of things, our struggles and triumphs are part of a much larger narrative. The pain we experience, though real and sometimes overwhelming, is temporary. God's eternal plan offers hope and redemption. Jesus' sacrifice on the cross and his resurrection provide us with the assurance that no matter what we face, God is with us and has a purpose for our lives.

When we shift our focus from finite to infinite, we become more resilient, more hopeful, and more committed to our faith. We understand that setbacks are not the end but part of the journey. God's story is long, and his people are everywhere. Be faithful and play your part. We will be okay. Our families will be okay. We are part of an infinite game that will last beyond our lives, and God holds it all in his hands. At just the right moment, the Lamb will appear and make all things right. Take heart, for he has overcome the world. Let us live with the confidence that comes from knowing we are part of God's eternal plan.

Reflect: Identify some investments you're making in eternity that will only fully pay off when we reach heaven.

50

Bringing Zombies to Life

Accompanying Scripture Reading: Matthew 28:1–10

JUST BEFORE JESUS DIED on the cross, he announced his victory:

> He said, "It is finished!" Then he bowed his head and gave up his spirit. (John 19:30)

The Greek word for "it is finished" is *tetelestai*, and it was used in three ways during Jesus' time. First, it was a financial term to announce that a debt had been paid. Second, it was a judicial term to announce that a punishment had been completed or that a sentence had been served. Third, it was a military term to announce that a victory had been won.[1] When Jesus died and was resurrected, he paid the debt of sin you couldn't pay, took the

---

1. Cortez and Howerton, "Significance behind Jesus' Last Words."

punishment your sin deserved, and won the victory over death that you couldn't win.

As proof of Jesus' victory over death, he didn't stay dead. Instead, he did the impossible: he rose from the dead. When Jesus' followers went to his tomb, they encountered an angel who declared Christ's victory over death. The great news is that Jesus' resurrection didn't only give him life. It also gave us life.

> He isn't here! He is risen from the dead, just as he said would happen. Come, see where his body was lying. (Matt 28:6)

My oldest son sleepwalks. When you look at him, he looks awake. However, when you start talking to him, you realize . . . no one's home. He is totally asleep. It is possible to look like you're awake but actually be asleep.

For me, it's after I faint. I am a fainter. When I get a shot, I faint. When I see my son after he gets his tonsils out, I faint. When I watch a violent movie, I faint. Lately, when I faint, it's really hard for me to wake up. Actually, my body wakes up, but my mind won't. I start to panic because I can't put a thought together. I don't know where I am or what's happening. I don't even know who I am. I'm awake, but I'm not awake. It is possible to look like you're awake but actually be asleep.

As a pastor, I've been at the bedside of several people when they have died. I've noticed something strange that happens at the moment they pass away. It's as if you can see their life leave them. You assume they'll just stop breathing and moving, but it's more than that. Their eyes might be open, but the life has left them.

So many of us spend our lives sleepwalking. We're hypnotized. I hear people call it depression, but for most people, it's just hopelessness. Depression is real for some, but a lot of people are just going through the motions. They've got video games, Netflix, shows, drugs, or activities, but there's no real life there.

And it's no surprise people are hopeless. The world desperately tries to convince you that life is hopeless. That's the world's agenda, but that's not how they say it, is it? They say the Big Bang was a random chance event. What does that mean? That means you're an accident, and you have no purpose.

You watch the news, and they spend almost twenty-four hours every day trying to convince you the world is worse off than it is. They focus on every little thing that is going wrong because if they can convince you the world is falling apart, their ratings increase.

They tell you to keep up with the Joneses, to look good and be successful. Then social media creates an impossible standard you could never possibly live up to. Everyone makes their lives look as perfect as possible, and we're all left thinking our lives are terrible compared to theirs. That's because we're comparing the worst parts of our lives to the highlight reels of their lives. Look at Hollywood. There are so many perfectly airbrushed, beautiful people there. You have no chance. If you compare yourself to that, of course, you'll be depressed.

Rich, powerful people dominate our X feed. So we compare our lives to theirs, and we just feel hopeless. The crazy thing is, they likely feel more hopeless than we do. So, what do we do about it? Well, you know I wouldn't be talking about it if God didn't offer us a solution to the problem.

Our church recently did a survey of our town and learned that people in Gillette are six times less likely to regularly feel hopeless if they regularly go to church. If that hasn't been your experience, it's likely because you didn't go deep enough or get connected to the church.

> Once you were dead because of your disobedience and your many sins. All of us used to live that way, following the passionate desires and inclinations of our sinful nature. By our very nature, we were subject to God's anger, just like everyone else. But God is so rich in mercy, and he loved us so much, that even though we were dead because of our sins, he gave us life when he raised Christ from the dead. (It is only by God's grace that you have been saved!) For he raised us from the dead along with Christ and seated us with him in the heavenly realms because we are united with Christ Jesus. (Eph 2:1–6)

Before you were a Christian, you were dead. This is as close to a description of a zombie as you can get. Your body was walking around, but internally you were dead. You were lifeless. Not only did our human nature cause us to live a lifeless, hopeless life, but it also kept us out of heaven. You were walking around dead in this life because you were destined for hell.

One clue you're sleepwalking is that you can sin without regretting it. If you can lie or lust without regretting it, you're asleep. If you can steal or hurt someone without regret, something is wrong with you. Jesus died to rescue you from that zombie life, and only Jesus can give you life.

Bringing Zombies to Life

You were dead because of sin, but sinning less can't bring you back to life. Sin caused death, but being good can't cause life. If cancer kills you, chemo can't bring you back to life. Only Jesus can give us life, and when he raises us to life, we leave the zombie life behind. Our life that was once filled with darkness is now filled with light, the light that's been lighting up our world since Jesus rose from the dead.

> The light makes everything visible. This is why it is said, "Awake, O sleeper, rise up from the dead, and Christ will give you light." (Eph 5:14)

Where does our light come from? Christ gives it to us. His resurrection allows us to be resurrected. It gives us life. Zombies, wake up! To be alive, we need four basic elements: water, air, food, and light. And what is Jesus? He is the living water, the breath of life, the bread of life, and the light of the world. We can't live without him. So what about you? Take an honest look at your life. Does your life come from Jesus?

The prodigal son decided to chase after all the things the world promised him would make him happy. He took half of his father's wealth and spent it on prostitutes, entertainment, drugs, and anything else he wanted. Eventually, he realized none of that gave him life and ran home to the only person who loved him unconditionally and who could actually give him the life he needed (Luke 15:11–32).

Jesus' resurrection proves that heaven is not a disappointment for which we'll have to settle. The resurrection means we can stop settling and start living. If you will run to Jesus, he will give you life.

Reflect: What are some ways to identify the people who are pretending to be alive and the people who are truly, spiritually alive?

51

Enduring Pain

Accompanying Scripture Reading: Matthew 28:11–20

My wife, Darci, grew up in a farming community called Sharon Springs, Kansas. There was only one small diner and one small grocery store, which means it was a table community. In Sharon Springs, life happens around the table. The pinnacle of life in Sharon is Christmas, and Darci's mom, Cathy, was the queen of Christmas. Decorations were everywhere, and the food was incredible. Cathy could cook, and it seemed we all gained fifty-five pounds every Christmas.

However, in 2008, the tradition was interrupted. While we were there, the house caught fire and burned down, right along with the new drill Darci's dad gave me for Christmas. It was a horrible experience, but the next Christmas was even worse. We had just found out that Darci's mom was really sick and couldn't pull off the normal Christmas celebration. A month

Enduring Pain

later, we found out she had stage four ovarian cancer. A few months later, she died on Mother's Day. So, Christmas 2010, in a rental house, without Cathy, wasn't a fun Christmas.

Darci's dad Kyle is the strongest man I've ever known. He carried the family, and amazingly, it actually drove him closer to God. This all happened the same year Darci and I got married, and even though it made our first few years of marriage really hard, it made our marriage stronger.

It's times like these that we start asking why a loving God would allow bad things to happen. When you ask that question, you're not thinking about not finding a good parking spot. You're thinking about something big—someone who died, or someone who left you. But God is not far from us when we ask these questions. In fact, God can relate to our pain. When we blame God, we point the finger in the wrong direction. We cause our pain. Adam and Eve caused our pain. Sinful people cause our pain, and sinful people cause God pain. God's chosen people killed his son, and on the cross, Jesus experienced incredible pain:

> At about three o'clock, Jesus called out with a loud voice, "Eli, Eli, lema sabachthani?" which means "My God, my God, why have you abandoned me?" (Matt 27:46)

The weight of all the world's sin was placed on Jesus' shoulders, and because he was now covered in the filth of sin, his Heavenly Father couldn't look at him. The Greek word for "called out" here is *aneboesen*, which means "to shout or scream." In this moment, Jesus is nailed to a cross, screaming in pain.

Jesus spent his life in intimate fellowship with his Father. Now, in his moment of greatest pain, his Father has abandoned him. The Greek word for abandoned here is *enkatelipes*, which means "to leave behind." In addition, almost everyone else in Jesus' life abandoned him too. Judas betrayed him. Peter denied him. His disciples couldn't stay awake to pray with him. The crowd turned on him, tortured him, and killed him.

Have you ever been rejected by someone you liked, by a friend, by a boss, or by a parent? Rejection is one of life's greatest pains. Jesus didn't scream because of the torture. He screamed because the pain of rejection was excruciating, but Jesus had to be abandoned so that we wouldn't have to be. There is now no rejection in the Christian faith. When you feel like God has abandoned you, know that if you are a child of God, he's right there with you in your pain.

The Life

After Jesus' resurrection, he gave his followers the Great Commission to go into the world and make disciples, but because the idea of continuing with the mission without Jesus was very scary to them, Jesus promised to be with them in spirit:

> I am with you always, even to the end of the age. (Matt 28:20)

You may feel alone, but God is with you. You may be in pain, but God is with you. You may feel abandoned, but God is with you.

If you're wondering why bad things happen, ask God. Take your hard questions to God. Sometimes when my kids ask me a hard question, I say, "I don't know, ask mom." Then she tells them to ask me. God doesn't do that. Go to God with bold questions. "God, why did this happen? Why did she die? Why didn't I get the job? Why the divorce, the cancer, the wars, slavery?" I believe that if we honestly bring our questions to God, he will give us peace.

What does the world think when they see someone enjoying pain? They think that person is crazy, but the apostle Paul says God gives us the power to do just that:

> We can rejoice, too, when we run into problems and trials, for we know that they help us develop endurance. And endurance develops strength of character, and character strengthens our confident hope of salvation. And this hope will not lead to disappointment. For we know how dearly God loves us because he has given us the Holy Spirit to fill our hearts with his love. (Rom 5:3–5)

Why do we rejoice? We know life is more than the chapter we're in. He'll give us hope and help us persevere. We can persevere because we know this season is a part of our story, not the entire story.

The struggle is going to make you better, and it's going to be a testimony God uses for good. Jesus died, but that was only part of his story. On the third day, he rose! The death is a testimony!

> Now we see things imperfectly, like puzzling reflections in a mirror, but then we will see everything with perfect clarity. All that I know now is partial and incomplete, but then I will know everything completely, just as God now knows me completely. (1 Cor 13:12)

What you're experiencing is a chapter in your autobiography. It's not the whole book. Someday we will be able to look back on our whole life and see how God worked it all together for good. God knows you so well that he knows your future. He can look forward and allow us to experience pain because he knows what it will produce.

Pain can be a great teacher. Ask God what lesson he plans to use your pain to teach you. If you want out of a season of pain, learn the lesson fast. If pain is meant to teach you, be a quick learner. Don't keep making the same mistake. Learn the lesson. Jesus did:

> Even though Jesus was God's Son, he learned obedience from the things he suffered. (Heb 5:8)

I don't think Jesus was born with all the knowledge he needed for his ministry. He spent years learning and maturing. Pain taught even Jesus.

The apostle Paul said he had a thorn in his flesh. Scripture never tells us what the thorn was. Some say it was a sin he wrestled with. Some say it was an illness or relationship issue. I believe it was that he wasn't picked to be the twelfth apostle that replaced Judas.

> Even though I have received such wonderful revelations from God. So to keep me from becoming proud, I was given a thorn in my flesh, a messenger from Satan to torment me and keep me from becoming proud. (2 Cor 12:7)

Paul claimed that Jesus spoke to him the same way he spoke to the twelve apostles. It felt like rejection from God, but it was actually God doing something in Paul.

So how do we persevere in our pain? We keep our eyes on Jesus:

> We do this by keeping our eyes on Jesus, the champion who initiates and perfects our faith. Because of the joy awaiting him, he endured the cross, disregarding its shame. Now he is seated in the place of honor beside God's throne. (Heb 12:2)

Jesus could persevere on the cross because he knew the mission. He knew his pain had a purpose. Your greatest pain can lead to your greatest ministry. If you want to know your calling, reflect on your pain. Our pain can reveal our calling. God doesn't usually cause our pain, but he uses it to lead us to our calling. We have new life because God used Jesus' pain, and God can use your pain too.

Let's return to the story of Jesus' crucifixion. Jesus has just screamed about God the Father rejecting him. Then he more fully gave himself to God:

> Then Jesus shouted, "Father, I entrust my spirit into your hands!" And with those words, he breathed his last. (Luke 23:46)

Don't let your pain lead you away from God; let it lead you to God.

> For all of God's promises have been fulfilled in Christ with a resounding "Yes!" And through Christ, our "Amen" (which means "Yes") ascends to God for his glory. (2 Cor 1:20)

Our cooperation with God's plan for our lives brings glory to God. Our "yes" ascends to God for his glory! Jesus was asked to go to the cross, and because he had greater knowledge of what was coming, he said yes.

So, what about you? Do you trust God in your pain?

Reflect: Did your moment of greatest pain lead you to God or away from him?

52

How to Be Powerful

Accompanying Scripture Reading: Acts 1:1–11

WHO WOULD YOU RATHER determine your life's agenda—God or you? Our world chooses to follow the desires of their flesh, but true joy comes when we surrender. Surrendering to God's will leads to a life of purpose and power beyond our imagination.

The last time anyone saw Jesus physically on earth is recounted in Acts 1, the story of Jesus' ascension to heaven. Imagine the disciples' emotions in those moments. Jesus, resurrected, stood before them. It had been forty days since Easter, and they had seen him several times. Yet, it still must have felt surreal. How often did they find themselves glancing at the holes in his hands and feet, marveling at this miracle standing before them?

Here they were, engaging in another deep conversation with Jesus, asking pressing questions. Then, suddenly, he was taken up into the sky. They were left standing there, awestruck. The disciples were likely still grappling with the reality of the resurrection, and now, Jesus was gone again, taken up into heaven. Yet, this was no surprise to Jesus. He had predicted it:

> Remember what I told you: I am going away, but I will come back to you again. If you really loved me, you would be happy that I am going to the Father, who is greater than I am. (John 14:28)

Jesus' ascension wasn't an ending, it was a transition. He was returning to the realms of heaven, not abandoning his followers but preparing a place for them. While we might wish for Jesus to stay physically present, God's plan required his departure so that he could send the Holy Spirit to us.

> Once when [Jesus] was eating with them, he commanded them, "Do not leave Jerusalem until the Father sends you the gift he promised, as I told you before. John baptized with water, but in just a few days you will be baptized with the Holy Spirit." So when the apostles were with Jesus, they kept asking him, "Lord, has the time come for you to free Israel and restore our kingdom?" He replied, "The Father alone has the authority to set those dates and times, and they are not for you to know." (Acts 1:4–7)

The disciples focused on an earthly kingdom and nearly missed the bigger picture. They asked about the restoration of Israel, still clinging to their expectations of a political Messiah, but Jesus redirected them, emphasizing the coming of the Holy Spirit. They were about to experience a new form of baptism—not a physical act but an immersion in God's presence and power. Jesus' mission was not about political liberation but about a spiritual revolution. He was preparing them for a task far beyond their imagination. When Jesus taught his disciples to pray, he instructed them to focus first on God as the king of an eternal kingdom:

> Our Father in heaven, may your name be kept holy. May your Kingdom come soon. May your will be done on earth, as it is in heaven. (Matt 6:9–10)

It is God's will that we are called to pursue, and his will is focused on his family. Jesus wanted his disciples to focus on the mission—making disciples of all nations. Their salvation was not just for them; it was also a mission.

Jesus ascended, but he did so with the promise that the Holy Spirit would come, empowering them to continue his work. The Holy Spirit's arrival marked a new era. Jesus, in his earthly form, could only be in one place at a time. Through the Holy Spirit, he could be present in every believer, everywhere. This was a game-changing moment. The Holy Spirit would empower believers, enabling them to carry out the mission Jesus had begun:

> But you will receive power when the Holy Spirit comes upon you. And you will be my witnesses, telling people about me everywhere—in Jerusalem, throughout Judea, in Samaria, and to the ends of the earth. (Acts 1:8)

The Greek word for "power" in this verse is *dunamis*, the root word for "dynamite." The Holy Spirit's arrival was like a spiritual explosion. It filled the disciples with a power that transformed them from fearful followers into bold witnesses:

> Suddenly, there was a sound from heaven like the roaring of a mighty windstorm, and it filled the house where they were sitting. Then, what looked like flames or tongues of fire appeared and settled on each of them. And everyone present was filled with the Holy Spirit. (Acts 2:2-4)

The Holy Spirit brings power, guidance, and transformation. He helps us to live righteous lives, gives us gifts to serve others, and empowers us to pray impactful prayers. The same power that raised Jesus from the dead lives in us, enabling us to be effective witnesses of his love and grace:

> The Spirit of God, who raised Jesus from the dead, lives in you. And just as God raised Christ Jesus from the dead, he will give life to your mortal bodies by this same Spirit living within you. (Rom 8:11)

God's agenda is far greater than our own. When we surrender our will to his, we become part of his grand plan to bring salvation to the world. This isn't about adding Jesus to our lives as a sidenote. This is about making him the center.

The Holy Spirit empowers us to be witnesses. A witness is someone who shares what they have seen, heard, and experienced. We are called to testify to the truth of Jesus Christ. The world needs this truth, and it needs us to boldly proclaim it.

When Jesus ascended, he didn't leave us alone. He sent the Holy Spirit to empower us to continue his work. We are part of a movement that spans the globe and the ages, empowered by the same Spirit that raised Jesus from the dead. Let's embrace this power, surrender our agendas, and fully commit to God's mission. Who would you rather determine your life's agenda—God or you? The answer should be clear. Let's choose God's agenda and witness the miraculous work he will accomplish through us.

Reflect: What courageous step is the Holy Spirit's powerful presence in your life leading you to take?

Conclusion

As you read this book, you may have noticed I missed some of the big events and teachings of Jesus. The truth is, I could have easily tripled the length of this book. John had the same struggle:

> *Jesus also did many other things. If they were all written down, I suppose the whole world could not contain the books that would be written. (John 21:25)*

I chose to focus on stories that would call us out of spiritual complacency and into deeper devotion. My prayer for you now is that you have a renewed passion to give yourself more fully to following Christ, that you will set your eyes on things above. However, my goal was not to guilt you into deeper devotion. The church has too often used pressure, fear, and shame to lead people to obedience, but Jesus used kindness:

> *Don't you see how wonderfully kind, tolerant, and patient God is with you? Does this mean nothing to you? Can't you see that his kindness is intended to turn you from your sin? (Rom 2:4)*

Heaven is not a reward for good works, but there will be rewards in heaven for those who do good things. There are consequences for sin and rewards for good works, but God's love is unconditional.

Do I love one of my sons more than the other if he is more obedient that day? No. If I do, it is only because I am not a perfect father. The other day we had a particularly hard day with disciplining Lincoln. That night when I was putting him to bed Lincoln asked me, "Dad, do you love me as much as you love Titus?" I nearly burst into tears. Before he asked this, I was frustrated, and my communication with him was not gentle. When I

CONCLUSION

realized what was happening, I told him, "I couldn't possibly love either of you any more than I already do, and I will never love you any less."

I may give Lincoln a reward for doing something good. I may discipline Titus for doing something bad, but that discipline is motivated by my love for them. They can't do anything to earn my love, and they can't do anything to take it away. I loved them when they were being formed in Darci's womb, and every night I tell my boys: "I love you forever and ever, no matter what."

God loved you into existence. You don't have to perform well to earn his love. Before you were born, your Heavenly Father sent his only son to die for you. You didn't do anything to earn it, but he died for you. Let that be your encouragement to give yourself more fully to him.

Acknowledgments

AT AN EARLY AGE, my dad, Roy Wilson, taught me not to simply accept the biblical interpretations of others but to explore deeper possibilities. Thank you, Dad.

As I read back through this book, I was struck by how much of it was influenced by the teachings of Leonard Sweet. His insights changed the way I think about the life of Jesus and taught me how to truly read the Bible. Thank you, Len.

My niece, Audrah Bartel, played a huge role in transforming my ramblings into a readable devotional. Thank you, Audrah.

My wife, Darci Wilson, sacrificed many hours to give me the space I needed to write this book. She is the most generous person I have ever known. I love you, Darci.

My sons, Lincoln and Titus, have unknowingly provided many of this book's illustrations. Boys, I love you. Thank you.

Bibliography

Barna Group. "Almost Half of Practicing Christian Millennials Say Evangelism Is Wrong." Barna, Feb. 5, 2019. https://www.barna.com/research/millennials-oppose-evangelism/.

Belling, Alasdair. "Going to Church Often Is Good for Your Mental Health." Undeceptions, Feb. 17, 2023. https://undeceptions.com/articles/going-to-church-is-good-for-your-mental-health/.

Bible Hub. "Strong's Greek: 4073. πέτρα (petra)." https://biblehub.com/greek/4073.htm.

———. "Strong's Greek: 4074. Πέτρος (Petros)." https://biblehub.com/greek/4074.htm.

———. "Strong's Greek: 4439. πύλη (pulé)." https://biblehub.com/greek/4439.htm.

———. "Strong's Greek: 5326. φάντασμα (phantasma)." https://biblehub.com/greek/5326.htm.

Bryan, Steve. "A Pool Strangely Stirred: The Healing at Bethesda in John 5." Tyndale House, June 14, 2024. https://tyndalehouse.com/explore/articles/the-healing-at-bethesda/.

Carmean, Kyle. "Sporus and Nero: The Controversial Union in Ancient Rome." History Defined. https://www.historydefined.net/sporus/.

Carse, James P. *Finite and Infinite Games: A Vision of Life as Play and Possibility*. New York: Ballantine Books, 1986.

"Child Mortality in the Greco-Roman World." Children in the Greco-Roman World. https://childreninthegrecoromanworld.omeka.net/exhibits/show/children/childmortality.

Cortez, Christa Gomes, and Josh Howerton. "The Significance behind Jesus' Last Words, 'It Is Finished.'" Christian Learning, June 7, 2024. https://www.christianlearning.com/jesus-last-words-it-is-finished/.

Daley, Jason. "Did the Ancient Greeks Engage in Human Sacrifice?" *Smithsonian Magazine*, Aug. 12, 2016. https://www.smithsonianmag.com/smart-news/did-ancient-greeks-engage-human-sacrifice-180960111/.

Edwards, Jonathan. "Sinners in the Hands of an Angry God." In *The Works of Jonathan Edwards*, edited by Sereno Dwight, 2:7–47. New York: G. & C. & H. Carvill, 1830.

"Effects of Religious Practice on Crime Rates." Marripedia. https://www.marripedia.org/effects_of_religious_practice_on_crime_rates.

Elder, Eric. "Lesson 9: What Happened at Caesarea Philippi?" *Ranch*, Nov. 8, 2010. https://theranch.org/2010/11/08/lesson-9-what-happened-at-caesarea-philippi/.

BIBLIOGRAPHY

Fisher, Kate, and Rebecca Langlands, eds. "Bestiality in the Bay of Naples: The Herculaneum Pan and Goat Statue." In *Sex, Knowledge, and Receptions of the Past*, 86–110. Oxford: Oxford University Press, 2015. https://doi.org/10.1093/acprof:oso/9780199660513.003.0005.

Foley, Ryan. "Practicing Christians Give More to Charity than Non-Christians: Study." Christian Post, Nov. 15, 2023. https://www.christianpost.com/news/practicing-christians-give-more-to-charity-than-non-christians.html.

Geggel, Laura. "How Do Palm Trees Withstand Hurricanes?" Live Science, Sept. 29, 2022. https://www.livescience.com/60393-why-palm-trees-are-so-flexible.html.

Golden, Mark. "PAIS, «CHILD» AND «SLAVE»." *L'Antiquité Classique* 54 (1985) 91–104. http://www.jstor.org/stable/41657155.

Griffin, Annette. "Did Jesus or the Pool of Bethesda Heal People?" Christianity.com, last updated Jan. 31, 2022. https://www.christianity.com/wiki/bible/did-the-waters-at-the-pool-of-bethesda-heal-or-does-jesus.html.

Guzik, David. "Study Guide for Acts 18." Blue Letter Bible. https://www.blueletterbible.org/Comm/guzik_david/StudyGuide_Act/Act_18.cfm.

Hansley, C. Keith. "Emperor Nero Had His Own Mother Killed." Historian's Hut, May 24, 2018. https://thehistorianshut.com/2018/05/24/emperor-nero-had-his-own-mother-killed/#:~:text=With%20the%20support%20of%20his,to%20prevent%20such%20an%20outcome.

Hudson, Abigail, and Ollie Burns. "LGBTQIA+ History Month—Male Homosexuality in Ancient Rome." *History @ Bham*, Feb. 8, 2021. https://blog.bham.ac.uk/historybham/lgbtqia-history-month-male-homosexuality-in-ancient-rome/.

Hulme, David. "Messiahs! Rulers and the Role of Religion, Part 1: Men as Gods." *Vision*, Spring 2005. https://www.vision.org/messiahs-rulers-religion-part-1-men-as-gods-709.

Jacobs, Shannon. "Meaning of Palm Branches in the Bible: What Do They Symbolize?" BibleKeeper. https://www.biblekeeper.com/palm-branches-meaning-in-the-bible/.

Jillette, Penn. "A Gift of a Bible." beinzee, YouTube, July 8, 2010. https://youtu.be/6md638smQd8.

Kumar, Anugrah. "60% of Adults under 40 Say Jesus Isn't Only Way to Salvation; Equal to Buddha, Muhammad." Christian Post, Aug. 22, 2021. https://www.christianpost.com/news/60-of-young-adults-say-jesus-isnt-the-only-way-to-salvation.html.

———. "Church Attendance Lowers Suicide Risk among US Women, Study Finds." Christian Post, July 2, 2016. https://www.christianpost.com/news/church-attendance-lowers-suicide-risk-among-us-women-study-finds.html.

Lewis, C. S. *The Four Loves*. New York: Harcourt Brace, 1960.

Lewis, Jone Johnson. "Poppaea Sabina: Nero's Mistress and Wife." ThoughtCo, last updated Apr. 18, 2019. https://www.thoughtco.com/poppaea-sabina-biography-3525460.

Lizorkin-Eyzenberg, Eli. "The Pool of Bethesda as a Healing Center of Asclepius." *Israel Institute of Biblical Studies*, Dec. 1, 2014. https://blog.israelbiblicalstudies.com/jewish-studies/bethesda-pool-jerusalem-shrine-asclepius/.

Lohnes, Kate. "Siege of Jerusalem." *Encyclopedia Britannica*, Aug. 29, 2018. https://www.britannica.com/event/Siege-of-Jerusalem-70.

Malik, Shushma. "Nero Versus the Christians." *History Today* 70:9 (September 2020). https://www.historytoday.com/archive/feature/nero-versus-christians.

BIBLIOGRAPHY

Oakes, John. "What Is the Evidence That Peter Was Crucified Upside Down in Rome?" Evidence for Christianity, Mar. 20, 2010. https://evidenceforchristianity.org/what-is-the-evidence-that-peter-was-crucified-upside-down-in-rome/.

Ortberg, John. *If You Want to Walk on Water, You've Got to Get Out of the Boat*. Grand Rapids: Zondervan, 2001.

Plato. *Euthyphro*. Translated by Harold North Fowler. Loeb Classical Library. Cambridge: Harvard University Press, 1914.

"Pool of Bethesda." *Friends of Conrad Schick*. https://conradschick.wordpress.com/archeology/pool-of-bethesda/.

Richter, Darmon. "11 Hidden Spots to Enter the Underworld." Atlas Obscura, Oct. 3, 2016. https://www.atlasobscura.com/articles/11-hidden-spots-to-enter-the-underworld.

Stanton, Glenn. "FactChecker: Divorce Rate among Christians." Gospel Coalition, Sept. 25, 2012. https://www.thegospelcoalition.org/article/factchecker-divorce-rate-among-christians/.

Steinmeyer, Nathan. "Biblical Monsters: Seven Mysterious Creatures of the Biblical World." *Biblical Archaeology Society*, July 20, 2023. https://www.biblicalarchaeology.org/daily/biblical-monsters/.

Stonestreet, John, and G. Shane Morris. "Dads, Take Your Kids to Church!" Christian Post, Mar. 16, 2019. https://www.christianpost.com/voice/dads-take-your-kids-church.html.

Tallis, Nigel. "Horses and Human History." *British Museum*, May 22, 2012. https://www.britishmuseum.org/blog/horses-and-human-history.

Tix, Andy. "The Science of Motivating Others." *Psychology Today*, Nov. 18, 2021. https://www.psychologytoday.com/intl/blog/the-pursuit-peace/202111/the-science-motivating-others.

Vander Laan, Ray. "Fertility Cults of Canaan." *That the World May Know*. https://www.thattheworldmayknow.com/fertility-cults-of-canaan.

———. "The Gates of Hell." *That the World May Know*. https://www.thattheworldmayknow.com/gates-of-hell.

Watts, Isaac. "Joy to the World." Hymnary, 1719. https://hymnary.org/text/joy_to_the_world_the_lord_is_come.

"We Are Stardust." American Museum of Natural History. https://www.amnh.org/exhibitions/permanent/the-universe/stars/a-spectacular-stellar-finale/we-are-stardust.

Zavada, Jack. "Who Were the Pharisees in the Bible?" Learn Religions, last updated Sept. 5, 2024. https://www.learnreligions.com/who-were-the-pharisees-700706.

Zuckerman, Patrick. "The Dead Sea Scrolls." Bible.org, Oct. 7, 2009. https://bible.org/article/dead-sea-scrolls.

www.ingramcontent.com/pod-product-compliance
Lightning Source LLC
Chambersburg PA
CBHW051049160426
43193CB00010B/1119